MW01181866

EXPLORING VITAL WORDS OF THE BIBLE

EXPLORING VITAL WORDS OF THE BIBLE

OF THE BIBLE

The 50 most Important
Words of the New Testament

J. M. FURNESS

WORLD
BIBLE PUBLISHERS, INC.
Iowa Falls, IA 50126 U.S.A.

TO MY PARENTS
W.F. and G.M.F.
In Affection and Gratitude

Exploring Vital Words of the Bible

Copyright© 1966 J.M. Furness

Previously published as *Vital Words of the Bible*

This edition is published by agreement of The Lutterworth Press, P.O. Box 60, Cambridge, CB1 2NT, England to whom all rights inquiries should be addressed.

Published in USA by World Bible Publishers, Inc., Iowa Falls, Iowa 50126.

ISBN 0-529-11278-7

Printed in the United States of America

1 2 3 4 5 6 BGP 06 05 04 03 02 01

LIST OF WORDS

ABBREVIATIONS

AV.   The Authorized Version of the Bible (1611).
Eng.   English.
EVV.   English Versions of the Bible.
Gk.   Greek.
Heb.   Hebrew.
LXX.   The Septuagint—the Greek translation of the Hebrew
       Old Testament, completed about 150 B.C.
Moff. James Moffatt, *A New Translation of the Bible*
       (1913-1924).
NEB.   The New English Bible (1961).
NT.   The New Testament.
OT.   The Old Testament.
RSV.   The Revised Standard Version of the Bible (1946-
       1952).
RV.   The Revised Version of the Bible (1881-1885).
RVm.   Marginal Reading in the Revised Version.

ABBREVIATION OF BIBLICAL BOOKS

Old Testament

Gen.	Genesis	Eccles.	Ecclesiastes
Ex.	Exodus	Is.	Isaiah
Lev.	Leviticus	Jer.	Jeremiah
Num.	Numbers	Lam.	Lamentations
Deut.	Deuteronomy	Ezek.	Ezekiel
Jos.	Joshua	Dan.	Daniel
Jud.	Judges	Hos.	Hosea
Ru.	Ruth	Ob.	Obadiah
1, 2 Sam.	1, 2 Samuel	Jon.	Jonah
1, 2 Kgs.	1, 2 Kings	Mic.	Micah
1, 2 Chr.	1, 2 Chronicles	Na.	Nahum
Ezr.	Ezra	Hab.	Habakkuk
Neh.	Nehemiah	Zeph.	Zephaniah
Est.	Esther	Hag.	Haggai
Ps.	Psalms	Zech.	Zechariah
Pro.	Proverbs	Mal.	Malachi

Apocrypha

1, 2 Esd.	1, 2 Esdras	Ecclus.	Ecclesiasticus
Wisd.	Wisdom of Solomon	1, 2 Macc.	1, 2 Maccabees

New Testament

Mt.	S. Matthew	1, 2 Thess.	1, 2 Thessalonians
Mk.	S. Mark	1, 2 Tim.	1, 2 Timothy
Lk.	S. Luke	Tit.	Titus
Jn.	S. John	Phn.	Philemon
Rom.	Romans	Heb.	Hebrews
1, 2 Cor.	1, 2 Corinthians	Ja.	James
Gal.	Galatians	1, 2 Pet.	1, 2 Peter
Eph.	Ephesians	1, 2, 3 Jn.	1, 2, 3 John
Phil.	Philippians	Ju.	Jude
Col.	Colossians	Rev.	Revelation

PREFACE

T H I S little volume does not pretend to be a full-scale theological word book, much less a Bible dictionary: it is, rather, an elementary and introductory study of some of the great words of the Bible, and an attempt to draw out the important religious truths which they contain.

Each study takes a Greek word as it occurs in the New Testament and briefly indicates first its use by pagan writers and in the common speech of New Testament times, and then the meaning of its Old Testament Hebrew equivalent, so that finally we can consider its significance for the apostolic writers, the background of whose thought is always partly Greek, and partly (often mainly) Hebraic. Because it is not the words themselves which matter, but the message of the inspired writers who used them, the Biblical references given are important: the best commentary on Holy Scripture is always Scripture itself!

In articles so short and condensed as these, there must of necessity be some omissions, and some points at which the treatment will appear too summary, but it is hoped that clarity has not been too often sacrificed to brevity, and that these pages will harvest a little, at least, of the present intensive study of Biblical theology for the benefit of local church workers, preachers and others, to whom the standard works of scholarship are not readily available. If it does this, if it stimulates an appetite for further study, if, above all, it serves to reveal in God's written word a little more of the redemptive love and living power of the Incarnate Word, Jesus Christ, it will have fulfilled its modest purpose.

A few suggestions for further reading are included.

Finally, two acknowledgements are due. Firstly, my dependence upon the great lexicons, word books, Bible dictionaries and standard theological works will be evident upon every page, and I gratefully own a very considerable debt. Secondly, my gratitude is due to the Proprietors of the religious journal, *Advance*, in which many of these articles first appeared under the title *Bible Keywords: A Guide for Local Preachers*. To them, and to the Editor, my friend, the Rev. A. S. Cresswell, M.A., I am grateful both for generous encouragement and for permission to reprint.

For the faults and shortcomings of the present volume, the author is, of course, entirely responsible.

J.M.F.

Leeds, 1965.

AGAPAN—TO LOVE

Greek has three main verbs meaning "to love": (i) *Eran*, used of sensual love (hence our "erotic") (ii) *Philein* ("philanthropy"), spontaneous, unreasoning affection for friends, homeland, etc. (iii) *Agapan* (very rare outside religious writings), a word which speaks of actions rather than emotions, and is free from the idea of enjoying or possessing its object. This is the verb used in Septuagint (LXX) to render the Heb. root *aheb*, and is the commoner NT word. The noun is *agapē*.

THE OLD TESTAMENT

Aheb is used for love in the widest sense:

1 Sensual love, passion (Gen. 25:28; Jud. 16:4; 2 Sam. 13:4; 1 Kgs. 11:1; Jer. 2:33).

2 Friendship, family affection (Gen. 22:2; Ex. 21:5; 1 Sam. 18:1).

3 Yahweh's love for Israel (and other nations), for the righteous, etc. This is a spontaneous love, grounded in His very nature, leading Him to undertake mighty acts of deliverance. It is also a holy love, making moral demands upon men (Deut. 4:37; 7:7ff.; 2 Chr. 2:11; Hos. 9:15; 11:1; Am. 5:15).

4 Man's love for Yahweh, His name, house, salvation, etc. (Ex. 20:6; Deut. 6:5; 1 Kgs. 3:3; Neh. 1:5; Ps. 26:8; 69:36; 70:4; 119:97).

5 Dutiful love of man for his neighbour, even his enemy (Lev. 19:18; Deut. 10:19; cf. Ex. 23:4f).

6 Uniquely among ancient religions, Heb. faith insists upon a reciprocal love between God and man, reflected in man's love for his fellow. But God's love comes first, with man's love as its response (Deut. 9:4ff.; Ezek. 16:3–14). In fact, God loves Israel not for what *it* is, but because of what *He* is.

Agapan is the commoner verb, though *philein* (Jn. 5:20; 1 Cor. 16:22; Rev. 3:19 etc.) also occurs, apparently with identical meaning (cf. Jn. 21:15ff.).

1 God's love revealed in providence, but more fully in Christ, and completed by men's love for each other (Jn. 3:16; 13:34; 17:26; Rom. 5:5-8; 2 Cor. 5:14; Gal. 2:20).

2 Man's love for God or Christ, **not spontaneous, but a** response to Divine love (1 Jn. 4:19). Implanted in the heart by God (Gal. 5:22; Eph. 3:16ff.), it displaces old, selfish love (Mt. 10:37; Lk. 16:13f; Jn. 12:25f; 15:19ff; 2 Tim. 3:2–5; Ja. 4:4; 1 Jn. 2:15).

3 Christian love for all men (Mt. 5:44; Mk. 12:33; Jn. 13:35; Eph. 5:2; 1 Thess. 4:9; 1 Pet. 1:22; 2:17; 1 Jn. 2:10), described in detail in 1 Cor. 13.

4 The fact that Christ can *command* love (Jn. 13:34) shows that it is **volitional as well as emotional**: it is, indeed, a way of life, the indispensable proof of our love for God (1 Jn. 4:20).

(See further A. Nygren, *Agape and Eros*; J. Moffatt, *Love in the New Testament*.)

ALĒTHEIA—TRUTH

In Homer, of the opposite to a lie, in later writers, of the opposite
to mere appearance, i.e. reality, the nature of things.

THE OLD TESTAMENT

Heb. nouns *emeth, emunah* and verb *aman* (from which we
get "amen"), mean steadfastness, reliability.

1 So God is the rock, a "God of faithfulness" (Deut. 32:4).
He keeps His covenant promises, and saves His people from
insecurity (Ps. 26:3; 31:5f; 93:5; 119:160). The dependability
of God is contrasted with the vanity of idols (Is. 41:29; Jer. 10:14;
cf. Ps. 31:6).

2 Truth is also required of man—he must seek it (Jer. 5:1),
speak it (Ps. 15:2) and walk in it (2 Kgs. 20:3). Man must have
truth "in the inward parts" (Ps. 51:6)—i.e. an unwavering
obedience to God's law.

THE NEW TESTAMENT

The Heb. idea of truth is still found—cf. Rom. 3:3-7, where
God's faithfulness is contrasted with human inconstancy, and
Jn. 17:17; 3 Jn. 3f, but the Gk. idea predominates. *Alētheia*
means not so much what is dependable, as the actual state of
affairs, things as they really are. Truth is the light which God in
Christ sheds on life, enabling man to know God and to know
himself (Jn. 8:12, 32). Men cannot discover truth by hard thinking—it is always *revealed* (Jn. 16:13) by the Spirit.

1 The truth is in Jesus (Jn. 1:14). Because He acts and speaks
in complete dependence on God, His word is true (Jn. 5:30; 8:
26), He *is* the truth (i.e. the faithful image of God)—Jn. 14:6,

13

the true bread, vine, etc. (Jn. 6:32f; 15:1), and His judgments are true because God is with Him (Jn. 8:16).

2   Man's knowledge of truth is not theoretical, but comes through encounter with Christ (Jn. 8:31f) which leads to salvation: indeed to be saved and to come to a knowledge of the truth are one and the same (1 Tim. 2:4). To know the truth is to be sanctified by it (Jn. 17:17f). Conversely, the disobedient are "ever learning", but "never able to come to the knowledge of the truth" (2 Tim. 3:7). Knowledge of truth is evidenced in life (Gal. 5:7; 1 Pet. 1:22); it is known by its fruit (1 Jn. 2:4ff). In short, truth is a practical thing—we are true as we are like Jesus, true to the pattern of manhood, and true to God's purpose in our creation.

ANGELOS—ANGEL

Messenger, envoy, one who announces or tells (Homer, Herodotus). In later philosophy and in magical and mystical writings, of semi-divine beings. In LXX, for Heb. *malak*.

Heb. *malak*, "messenger", "agent", EVV "angel".

I Of God Himself. In early popular writings, "The angel of God" or "of the LORD" (Gen. 31:11–13; Ex. 3:2–6; Jud. 6:11ff; 31:21f etc.) is not an angel in the common sense, but God Himself appearing in human form: the appearances are theophanies, as the narratives make clear.

II Of angels proper:

1 Spiritual beings, inferior to God but superior to men, called also *elohim* (Ps. 8:5; 82:1; 138:1, etc.), *bene el(oh)im*—"sons of God" (Gen. 6:2; Job 1:6; 2:1; Ps. 29:1; 89:6), *qadoshim =* "saints" (AV), "holy ones" (RV) (Job 5:1; Ps. 89:5; Dan. 4:17; Zech. 14:5, etc.), "the host of heaven" (1 Kgs. 22:19), "the host of the height" (Is. 24:21). These attend and worship God in the heavenly court (1 Kgs. 22:19ff; Neh. 9:6; Ps. 29:1; 103:20; Is. 6:3) and occasionally appear on Earth (Gen. 28:12; 32:1). Sometimes they prove disobedient and invoke God's punishment (Gen. 6:2–4, cf. 2 Pet. 2:4; Jude 6; Job 4:18; 21:22; Is. 34:4f).

2 Normally angels are invisible, fiery beings (Jud. 13:20; 2 Kgs. 6:17; Ps. 104:4; Dan. 10:6), and certain classes are mentioned—*irin* ("watchers": Dan. 4:17), *seraphim* (lit. "burning ones": Is. 6:2, 6), *cherubim* (which probably have an animal form: Ps. 18:10; Ezek. 9:3).

3 In later Heb. thought, which emphasized God's transcendence rather than His immanence, the felt need for intermediaries between God and man brought angels, as His agents or messengers, into greater prominence (cf. Ezek. 40:3; Zech. 2). They

bring God's help (Ps. 91:11; Dan. 3:28; cf. Heb. 1:14), and His revelation (1 Kgs. 13:18; Dan. 10:11; Zech. 4:1-7; cf. Mt. 1:20; Acts 10:3), as well as man's intercession (Job 5:1; Zech. 1:12). They are also the heralds of God's judgment (Gen. 19:11f; Num. 22:22f; 2 Kgs. 19:35; Ps. 78:49ff etc.)

4 In the latest books of the canon (e.g. Daniel, Zechariah), some angels have personal names, e.g. Michael, Gabriel, and in the apocryphal writings the doctrine of angels is further elaborated, and practically all God's communication with men is through these spiritual intermediaries. In this period, the "sons of God" of Gen. 6:2-4 are seen as fallen angels, headed by Satan, so that we have also a developing demonology. In all this, Persian influence (strong after the Exile) has worked on very ancient Israelitish notions of angelic beings and on the growing awareness of God's "otherness", which made direct divine contact with men seem incongruous. The angels brought in to bridge the gulf are, however, very much created and subordinate beings: God's uniqueness and authority are maintained, and we nowhere find the outright dualism typical of Persian religion.

5 Nevertheless, though angelology became well established in popular religion (e.g. in the Dead Sea Scrolls), the official priestly tradition remained adamant against it, and even in books as late as Ecclesiasticus, Wisdom, Maccabees and Psalms of Solomon, angels are rarely mentioned.

THE NEW TESTAMENT

Angels are now firmly established in popular theology (though the conservative Sadducees remain sceptical—Acts 23:8) and their existence can be taken for granted, but there is no speculation about their precise nature.

1 They play a rôle as divine agents in the Nativity (Mt. 1:20ff; 2:13; Lk. 1:11ff, 26ff; 2:9ff) and Resurrection (Mt. 28:2ff; Mk. 16:5ff; Lk. 24:4ff, 23; Jn. 20:12f) and in the spiritual struggles of Jesus in the Temptation (Mt. 4:11; Mk. 1:13) and the Agony (Lk. 22:43). In Acts they signify God's continuing

activity in furthering the work of the Church (Acts 5:19; 8:26; 10:3; 12:7; 27:23 etc.).

2 Angels are frequently mentioned as members of the heavenly court (Mk. 12:25; Lk. 12:8; 15:10; 16:22; Jn. 1:51; Gal. 1:8, etc.), and as God's warriors (Mt. 24:31; 26:53), while Mt. 18:10 seems to speak of guardian angels.

3 Angelic beings, though associated with, and employed by, God are not in any sense divine, and are not to be made the objects of prayer or worship (Col. 2:18; Rev. 22:8). Christ is superior to the angels (Heb. 1:4ff), and even the believer, because he is a son, enjoys a fellowship with God denied to them, who are only His servants (1 Cor. 6:3; 1 Pet. 1:12; cf. Jn. 15:15). Indeed, the fellowship of the believer with God through Christ and the Holy Spirit needs no angelic intermediary (Gal. 3:19).

4 Wicked angels, "angels of Satan" (Mt. 25:41; 2 Cor. 12:7; cf. Rev. 9:11; 12:7) are heavenly beings who have rebelled, and are enemies alike of God and men (cf. Rom. 8:38; Eph. 6:12; Jude 6): there are spiritual forces of evil to be reckoned with, but the final victory is God's.

5 The Angels of the Church (Rev. 2–3) may be (a) messengers sent by the churches to John, (b) the bishops who oversee the several churches, (c) their protective guardian angels. Most likely they represent only the heavenly counterpart of the earthly fact that, as Christians, our life is "hid with Christ in God".

(E. Langton, *The Angel Teaching of the NT*)

ANTHRŌPOS—MAN

Of man as an individual, and generally of the human race
(Homer, Plato, al.). The Eng. derivative is *anthropology*. In LXX
chiefly for Heb. *adam* and *ish*, also for *enosh* (pl. *anashim*).

Of the three Heb. words, *adam* (probably from *adamah*=the
ground) which means a human being as such (Gen. 2:5; Jer.
21:6), or mankind collectively (Gen. 1:26; Job 5:7), is the most
important religiously. Only in the creation myth is *Adam* a
proper name, and even there he clearly symbolizes humanity.

1 Man, as creature, is clearly distinguished from God (1 Sam.
15:29; Is. 17:7; 31:3): as the only creature made in the image and
likeness of the Creator, he is equally distinct from the animals,
and the distinction is to be rigorously observed (Lev. 18:23;
20:15).
2 The doctrine of the image and likeness implies that man,
made of the dust of the earth, nevertheless shares the divine
qualities of creative ability, understanding, moral sense, free
will, etc., because God has breathed into him the breath of life
(Gen. 2:7). Indeed, the breath (or spirit—*ruach*) of God within
him is the source of all man's lofty attributes (*see* SPIRIT).
This is one aspect of the Biblical view of man: he is superior to
all other creatures, and, as God's vicegerent, is curator of the
Earth and steward of its resources (Gen. 2:15; Ps. 8:5ff).
3 But man, not content with his creaturely status, aspired to
equality with his Maker, and this is the other, and darker, aspect
of human nature. The myth of Gen. 3 shows how, when man
rebelled against God, nature rebelled against him (Gen. 3:17ff).
Once man denied his creaturely status, his character degenerated
(Gen. 6:5), human relations were perverted (Gen. 4), and the
whole economy of nature disrupted. Even after a fresh start

with Noah, human pride reasserted itself, and led to the dispersal of the nations and a confusion of tongues which was reversed only by the pouring out of the Spirit at Pentecost (cf. Gen. 11 and Acts 2).

4 Although, through disobedience, God's image in man was defaced, it was not obliterated: man is degenerate, but not totally depraved. He is still a moral agent, capable of being reformed, which is the point of God's sustained moral appeal through Law and Prophets (Deut. 30:19; Ps. 51:7ff; Is. 1:18ff).

THE NEW TESTAMENT

The word *anēr*, a man or husband, which in LXX generally stands for *ish* or *enosh*, occurs frequently, mostly of individual men, but the important word is *anthrōpos*—man as he is in relation to God and the animals.

1 Man is a creature entirely dependent upon God's providence (Mt. 6:26–30; Acts 17:28): as God's son (Lk. 3:38), he has a peculiar dignity and his soul a supreme worth (Mt. 10:30f; 16:26; Lk. 10:20; 15). Nevertheless, men are only potentially and ideally God's children; true sonship is the status only of those who are in a right relationship with the Father (Mt. 5:9, 45; Jn. 1:12).

2 All humanity, as created, is one blood (Acts 17:26), but in fact there are racial and national barriers which are broken down only by acceptance of the Gospel (Gal. 3:28).

3 Man is everywhere in revolt: he has turned from God, and through an arrogant desire for independence, has wrought his own moral ruin (Rom. 1.21ff). This is not total depravity, for man remains morally responsible: even natural man, outside the Gospel, has a law written in his heart (Rom. 2:15), and conscience is as universal as sin.

4 But conscience is powerless to save, and unregenerate man is a walking civil war (Rom. 7:21ff); sin has so enslaved the heart and perverted the judgment that man as he is is but a caricature of what he was intended to be. Indeed, there is only one real man, Jesus, whose perfect humanity is obvious even to the moral confusion of Pilate (Jn. 19:5).

5 It is through the perfect man, Jesus, that a new humanity

becomes possible (Jn. 3:14–16; 2 Cor. 5:17): just as Christ inaugurates a new Covenant for the New Israel, so by His obedience, which cancels the disobedience of Adam (cf. Phil. 2. with Gen. 3), He ushers in a new humanity (Rom. 5:18f). Through the first Adam, Paradise was lost: through the last Adam, Christ, it is regained (1 Cor. 15:22, 45), but only by those who are "in Christ"—i.e. have responded to Him in repentance and faith.

6 In Pauline theology, as we have seen, physical death was the penalty of man's sin (Rom. 5:12–14; 1 Cor. 15:21), though Gen. 3:19 need not imply that man, as originally created, was immortal. It may be that man, had he not sinned, would have become immortal, but that is mere speculation. The fact is that he did sin and thereby lost his moral qualities in a spiritual death. Whether physical mortality was entailed by sin or not, the fact of NT theology is that in Christ fallen man can be reborn by the Spirit (Jn. 3:3), and that not just to life, but to life eternal (v. 15).

(H. W. Robinson, *The Christian Doctrine of Man*; E. Brunner, *Man in Revolt*; R. Niebuhr, *The Nature and Destiny of Man*)

APHIENAI—TO FORGIVE

Like the other Biblical words for forgiveness, *aphienai* is a metaphor. Its central meaning is "send or put away", hence "set free" (Thucydides), "acquit", "remit" (of a charge: Herodotus) or "excuse". In LXX for *nasa, salach* etc.

THE OLD TESTAMENT

Though a host of different metaphors are used—e.g. "blot out" (Ps. 51:1; Is. 43:25), "cleanse" (Jer. 33:8; Ez. 37:23), "forget" (Ps. 25:7; Jer. 31:34) etc., the chief Heb. words are *kaphar* (lit. "cover"—i.e. put out of sight: Ps. 78:38; Jer. 18:23), *nasa* ("lift up", "carry away"—i.e. remove the barrier of sin: Num. 14:19; Ps. 25:18), *salach* ("let go", "send away"—i.e. dismiss from mind: Ps. 103:3; Amos 7:2). *Nasa* is used both of divine and human (Gen. 50:17; 1 Sam. 25:28) forgiveness, *kaphar* and *salach* only of the former.

1 To obtain human forgiveness, the offender must make restitution, followed by a service of atonement (Lev. 6:2–7: *see* THÜSIA Sacrifice). Even in case of sins of ignorance, repentance and sacrifice must precede forgiveness (Lev. 4:13ff; Num. 15:23ff).

2 Because God is holy, and must therefore take a grave view of sin, His forgiveness is possible only when men humble themselves and repent (2 Chr. 7:14; Ps. 86:5). Men must determine to amend, and turn towards God (i.e. be converted) if they would be pardoned (Jos. 24:19ff; 2 Kgs. 24:4; Jer. 5:1, 7; Ezek. 18:30–32). It is this need for repentance which John Baptist emphasized (Mk. 1:4), and which Jesus demanded as the condition of entry to the Kingdom (Mk. 1:15). Pardon and forgiveness are not just an exercise of God's prerogative, but a natural expression of His love which *wants* to forgive (Neh. 9:17; Dan. 9:9; Jer. 36:3), and when man repents and turns to God, there is no limit to His pardoning love (Deut. 30:1–10; 1 Kgs. 8:36–50; Ps. 103:8–17).

The verb is used in various other of its classical senses—"leave, forsake" (Mt. 4:11; Mk. 7:8); "send away, divorce" (1 Cor. 7.11–13); "suffer, allow, permit" (Mt. 3:15; Jn. 12:7), but its significance is in relation to forgiveness. It occurs almost exclusively in Gospels and Acts; Paul almost invariably uses another verb, *CHARIZESTHAI* (from *charis*=grace), with identical meaning.

1 Forgiveness is a Divine prerogative (Mt. 6:14f; Mk. 11:25f; Lk. 23:34), and though Jesus claims the power to forgive sins (Mt. 9:2; Mk. 2:10; Lk. 5:20), He seems to have regarded it as delegated from the Father. This is seen clearly in the Epistles, where forgiveness is frequently described as "in" or "through" Christ (Eph. 4:32; 1 Jn. 2:12; Rev. 1:5, etc.).

2 For God to forgive, there must be some moral likeness between man and God (Mt. 5:43–48): that man only who has the merciful and loving spirit which forgives a wrong (and goes on forgiving without limit: Mt. 18:20f) can receive forgiveness (Mt. 6:12, 15; 18:23ff; Mk. 11:26; Lk. 17:4). Forgiveness is a gift to be enjoyed and *shared*!

3 Forgiveness is closely connected with Christ's death, the redemptive act which makes remission of sins possible (Mt. 26:28; Mk. 10:45; Heb. 9:15, 22. *See DIKAIOUN—JUSTIFY*). Therefore the Church preaches forgiveness and grants it in the name of Christ (Acts 2:38; 10:43; 13:38; Eph. 1:7; Col. 1:14; Ja. 5:15; 1 Jn. 2:12: cf. the commission to the disciples: Mt. 16:19; 18:18; Lk. 24:47; Jn. 20:23). In conformity with Jesus' teaching, the practice of forgiveness is a requirement and consequence of God's pardon: the rule is "freely ye have received, freely give" (Eph. 4:32; Col. 3:13).

4 There is no limit to God's forgiveness save that set by the perversity of spirit which chooses to call light darkness (the "blasphemy against the Holy Spirit": Mk. 3:28–30 and parallels; cf. Heb. 10:26): only the obstinate heart and perverse will of man can preclude God's loving pardon, and this alone is the "sin unto death" (1 Jn. 5:16).

BAPTISMA—BAPTISM

This word, not found in classics or LXX, describes the state resulting from the action of the verb *baptizein*. The verb means to dip, immerse, sink (Polybius), or, metaphorically, to swamp, as when refugees inundate a city (Josephus). *Baptizein* is used by late writers of pagan baptism, and in LXX with the meaning, dip (e.g. of Naaman; 2 Kgs. 5:14).

According to the Mishnah (a compilation of rabbinic teaching, c. 200 A.D.), Jews baptized their proselytes, but it is not altogether clear whether this was a ritual cleansing of the Gentile convert, or an initiation rite incorporating him into the religious nation.

THE NEW TESTAMENT

I. John's Baptism. The description of John as "the baptizer" (*ho baptizōn*: Mk. 1:4; 6:14, 24) and "the baptist" (*ho baptistēs*: Mk. 6:25; Lk. 7:20 etc.) may indicate the novelty of the rite he used. His baptism, by immersion in Jordan, was an eschatological rite of incorporation into the new age of the immanent Messiah (Lk. 3:15ff; Jn. 1:26), a means of escaping "the wrath to come" (Lk. 3:7), and demanded repentance (Mt. 3:6) and good works (Lk. 3:8, 10–14). Though John thought of his ministry as preparatory and incomplete, his baptism, uncompleted by the Christian rite, was known and continued to be practised in Alexandria and Ephesus for a generation (Acts 18:25; 19:1–7). Jesus' submission to John's baptism (Mt. 3:13ff) signified approval of John's work, and shewed the continuity between the Baptist's ministry and His own, and the vicarious rite both indicated His solidarity with sinful humanity, and marked Him as the Lamb of God (Jn. 1:29–34), thus anticipating the sacrificial death which He will later describe as "a baptism" (Mk. 10:38; Lk. 12:50).

II. Christian Baptism.

1 Jesus did not baptize (Jn. 4:2), and probably His disciples

were commanded to do so only after His death and Resurrection had completed the work of salvation. Mt. 28:19f is a word of the Risen Lord, and the inclusion of a Trinitarian formula suggests later liturgical usage, while Mk. 16:15, also post-Resurrection, is omitted by the earliest manuscripts.

2 Though it is not (like the eucharist) traced back to an institution by Jesus, baptism in His name, which is a baptism of repentance with a view to pardon, is in Acts the universal and indispensable means of admission to the church (Acts 2:38–41; 9:18; 19:5, etc.), and seems to have been the earliest sacrament.

3 Baptism is always associated with the Holy Spirit, the gift of which sometimes precedes immersion (Acts 10:44–48; 11:15–18); at other times, baptism comes first, the Holy Spirit being imparted by subsequent laying on of hands (Acts 8:14ff). Baptism of adults (male and female) upon confession of faith (Acts 8:36f; 1 Tim. 6:12; cf. Heb. 10:2) was the rule, and infant baptism is nowhere specifically mentioned, though it may be inferred from the baptism of whole households (Acts 16:15; 1 Cor. 1:16).

4 Acts 8:38; 9:18 indicate that baptism was not an exclusively apostolic function: Paul regarded it as subsidiary to his preaching, and 1 Cor. 1:14–17 taken with Acts 18:8 and 1 Cor. 16:16 suggests that he baptized only the first believers in a town, leaving local church leaders to baptize subsequent converts.

5 Theologically, baptism is the outward sign of God's work of grace in the heart, and is so real that it can be said to save (1 Pet. 3:21), and can be received by believers vicariously to gain the benefits of Christ's death for those who died without having heard the Gospel (1 Cor. 15:29f). It is a washing away of sins (Acts 22:16; 1 Cor. 6:11; Eph. 5:26), the death (as it were, by burial or drowning) of the old nature, and regeneration (Tit. 3:5; cf. Jn. 3) of a new life. Thus the believer can be said to have been baptized into Christ's death and Resurrection (Rom. 6:3ff; Col. 2:12) and incorporated into His life (Gal. 2:20; Phil. 1:20). The believer who has now "put on Christ" (Gal. 3:27) or "the new man" (Eph. 4:24) and is "in Christ" (Rom. 6:11; 1 Cor. 1:30 etc.), is sealed as belonging to God, and has the Holy Spirit as the guarantee of his new status (2 Cor. 1:22; 5:5). Henceforth he lives a new and higher life (Col. 3:1–15; Heb.

10:19–25; cf. 1 Cor. 10:1–14). In fact, by baptism, the believer has been born by water and the spirit, and has entered the Kingdom of God.

(H. G. Marsh, *The Origin and Significance of the NT Baptism*; O. Cullmann, *Baptism in the NT*)

BASILEIA—KINGDOM

Properly kingly rule, reigns, sovereign power, dominion, rather than kingdom in the territorial sense.

THE OLD TESTAMENT
Heb. *malekuth, mamlakah.*

1 Of earthly kingdoms, especially Israel or (after Solomon) Israel and Judah (Deut. 3:4; Jos. 11:10; 1 Kgs. 4:21; 2 Kgs. 14:5).

2 Of Yahweh's sovereignty or dominion. Heb. thought is theocratic: Yahweh is supreme, sovereign ruler (Ex. 15:18; 1 Chr. 28:5; Neh. 9:35; Ps. 22:28; 103:19; Is. 37:20; Dan. 4:34), and He appoints and removes earthly monarchs (1 Sam. 13:14; 1 Kgs. 11:11; 19:15f).

3 Men may scorn God's sovereignty, but nevertheless it will be catastrophically demonstrated in the Day of the Lord (*see HĒMERA*) with the advent of the Messiah-King (Is. 9:6f; 11:1–20; Zeph. 3:8f, etc.).

4 After the Exile (586-538 B.C.), one strain of prophecy expects the nations to be gathered into the kingdom (Is. 19: 18–25; 42:1–4; 49:1–6; 52:13–53:12; 66:18f; cf. Ps. 87 and Jonah); the other sees Israel only as the kingdom, with other nations either destroyed or in subservience (Hag. 2:6, 22; Zech. 12:6).

THE NEW TESTAMENT
1 Jesus announces the coming of the Kingdom, the fulfilment of OT expectation (Mt. 13:17); it is present in the midst of men (Lk. 17:21 RVm), and Christ's power over evil spirits is a sign of its having come (Lk. 11:20). Jesus' teaching is contained mainly in the first three Gospels (the *Synoptics*): John does not make much use of "kingdom", using instead "life" (*zōē*) with

much the same meaning. Even in Synoptics "life" and "kingdom" can be synonymous (cf. Mk. 9:43; 45 and Mk. 9:47).

2 The Kingdom is absolute in its claims, and demands undivided loyalty (Lk. 9:62; cf. Mt. 6:24; 10:37). Entry to the Kingdom is costly (Mt. 19:12; Mk. 9:43–47; Lk. 9:60), but well worth the surrender of all else (Mt. 13:44–46).

3 It is not built by men, but given by God (Lk. 12:32) and received or inherited by men (Mk. 10:15; Mt. 25:34; cf. Heb. 12:28).

4 Entry is by repentance and faith (Mk. 1:15), childlike trust (Mt. 18:3f), rebirth (Jn. 3:3–5), and is denied to the unrighteous (1 Cor. 6:9).

5 The coming of Christ is a crisis (Gk. *krisis*=judgment), and calls for watchfulness and quick decision (Mt. 25:1–3; Lk. 16:1–8; 12:58f).

6 The Kingdom is both present and future: it is here in germinal form, inaugurated by Christ's coming, and grows quietly but inexorably towards its completion (Mk. 4:26ff; 4:30ff; cf. Mt. 13:24ff), which takes place at the second coming.

7 Not lip-service to Christ, but humble obedience will admit us to the Kingdom (Mt. 7:21ff)—we can only pray "Thy Kingdom come" when we are prepared to say "Thy will be done".

(C. H. Dodd, *The Parables of the Kingdom*; J. Jeremias, *The Parables of Jesus*, 89ff)

CHARA—JOY

In the tragedians, Plato (frequently), inscriptions and papyri, of joy and delight in a quite general sense, and, by metonymy, of their cause or occasion.

THE OLD TESTAMENT

1 Joy is the natural product of a normal, healthy relationship between man and God, and is therefore characteristic of the believer. Cf. Ps. 1:1; 32:1; 84:4; 128:1, where "blessed" (Heb. *ashere*=blessed, happy) means "O, the happiness of . . .". The chief equivalents of *chara* are *simchah* (gladness, mirth) and *sason* (joy, gladness).

2 Yahweh rejoices over His creative work (Ps. 104:31) and in restoring and saving His people (Deut. 30:9; Is. 62:5; Zeph. 3:17).

3 Men rejoice in God's faithfulness and saving love (Ps. 16:11; Is. 12:3; Jer. 15:16; 33:11, etc.), and ecstasy is a characteristic of cultic worship (Neh. 12:43; Ps. 27:6).

4 Man's delight in Yahweh is accompanied by observance of the Law and ritual sacrifice, and so involves will as well as feeling (Deut. 12:7-12; Ps. 119, etc.).

5 The Day of the Lord, when the sovereignty of Yahweh will be universally recognized, is the supreme occasion of joy (Is. 35; 65:17-19; Zech. 9:9; cf. Ps. 96:7-13).

THE NEW TESTAMENT

1 The Messianic expectation is realized in the birth of Jesus Christ, which therefore occasions rejoicing (Mt. 2:10; Lk. 1:47; 2:10).

2 Peter is described as "happy" (*makarios*) when he recognizes Jesus (Mt. 16:17); Jesus rejoices over the success of His ministry, which ushers in the Kingdom (Mt. 13:16; Lk. 10:17); God rejoices over the recovery of sinners (Lk. 15:7, 10).

3 Joy characterizes the Church in Acts, especially in the success of evangelism (Acts 8:8; 13:48; 15:3).

4 In Epistles, joy is a fruit of the Spirit (Gal. 5:22; cf. Rom. 14:17), and a mark of Christians, especially in adversity (Phil. 1:18; 4:4).

5 Indeed, Christians may rejoice in persecution, knowing that they share their Lord's suffering, and that the trials herald the end of the Age (Mt. 5:12; Rom. 5:3ff; 12:12; 2 Cor. 6:10; Col. 1:24; 1 Pet. 1:6–12; 4:13). Joy, then, is both a present experience and an eschatological hope.

CHARIS—GRACE

In objective sense, beauty, attractiveness; subjectively of favours given or received, and the kindness and goodwill which prompt, or the gratitude which results from them. Concretely of the favour itself, a boon, delight, gratification.

THE OLD TESTAMENT

Heb. *chen*, grace, favour: not a thing, but an *attitude*.

1 Human favour (Gen. 34:11; Ruth 2:2; 2 Sam. 14:22).

2 Especially of God's graciousness to men, free, unmerited, given by a superior to inferiors quite irrespectively of any bond or covenant between them. So Noah finds grace in God's sight before there is any mention of covenant (Gen. 6:8).

3 God's grace is shown by care, protection and deliverance of His people, and by His free forgiveness (Ex. 33:13ff; Jud. 6:16f; Jer. 31).

4 Grace evokes from men repentance and prayer (Zech. 12:10).

Chen never rises to the heights of the NT doctrine of *charis*; indeed, the theological equivalent of *charis* in the OT is *chesed*=goodness, loving-kindness, mercy, and it is there rather than in *chen* that the roots of the doctrine of grace are found.

(See under ELEOS—MERCY. On *Chen* and *Chesed*, see N. H. Snaith, *The Distinctive Ideas of the Old Testament* (1950), 94–130.)

THE NEW TESTAMENT

1 The grace of God is shown supremely in Christ who both *is*, and *bestows*, *charis* (Jn. 1:1–17; Acts 15:11; Rom. 1:5; 2 Thess. 1:12). Grace is indeed the whole gospel, the good news

(Acts 13:43; 20:24; 2 Cor. 6:1ff; Col. 1:6), and includes justification, forgiveness, redemption from sin (Rom. 6:1; 2 Cor. 8:9; 1 Tim. 1:14ff). The phrase "grace and peace" in the greetings and blessings of the epistles is understood in this sense.

2 Since all salvation is of grace (even man's response!— 1 Cor. 15:10; Gal. 1:15; cf. Acts 5:31), and quite unmerited, human boasting is excluded (Rom. 3:27; 1 Cor. 1:31; Eph. 2:9).

3 Even Divine grace may be received in vain, i.e. without resulting Christian virtue (2 Cor. 6:1). The truth is that while God's grace initiates man's salvation, man must persevere in faith and good works if he is to grow in grace (Phil. 3), working out his own salvation (Phil. 2:12ff). Grace does not replace human effort and endurance but inspires, enlarges and transforms it (cf. 2 Cor. 3:5; 12:9f; Phil. 4:13).

(John Oman, *Grace and Personality*, Fontana Library.)

CHRISTOS—CHRIST, MESSIAH

Properly an adjective, "to be rubbed on", used as an ointment or salve.

Heb. *mashiach*, "anointed".

1 Kings, priests and prophets were anointed with oil to qualify them for office (e.g. Saul, 1 Sam. 10:1; Aaron, Ex. 29:7; Elisha, 1 Kgs. 19:16), hence "anointed" came to mean someone set apart for a particular office. Thus in 1 and 2 Sam. "his", "my", "the Lord's anointed" is the king, usually Saul; in Ps. 105:15, the patriarchs are meant; in Hab. 3:13, Israel; in Is. 45:1, Cyrus; in Dan. 9:25, Cyrus or the High Priest, Joshua.

2 *Mashiach* is never used of a divine prince to be raised up at some future time; Messianic ideas are there (e.g. Is. 9:6f; 11:1–5), but the word is not used. Messianic ideas are a development of nationalistic ideas of ideal kingship (esp. Davidic kingship), but Messiah is always God's servant or agent, never His equal.

3 In the popular mind of Jesus' time, Messiah was expected to restore the national fortunes of Israel (Lk. 24:21; Acts 1:6ff), though the pious cast him in a more spiritual rôle (Lk. 2:25f).

THE NEW TESTAMENT
1 Of the expected Jewish Messiah (Mt. 2:4; Lk. 2:11, 26).

2 Of Jesus recognized as Messiah (Mk. 8:29; Jn. 1:20; Acts 2:36; 4:26). In the Synoptics, Jesus is only gradually recognized, whereas in the Fourth Gospel, He is hailed as Christ from the beginning of His ministry.

3 Whether Jesus unequivocally declared Himself to be Christ is not easy to say (cf. Mt. 26:63f; Mk. 14:61f; Lk. 22:67ff; Jn.

4:25f); probably He thought of Himself in terms of Messiah modified by Suffering Servant ideas (see DOULOS), and certainly he preferred the title "Son of Man".

4 In Epistles, *Christos, Christos Iēsous, Iēsous Christos*, is a proper name. Gentiles, not greatly interested in Jewish ideas, may have taken *Christos* as if it were *chrēstos* (good, kind, gracious).

5 Jesus certainly fulfilled the greatest Messianic hopes, but He far surpasses anything implied in the hope or the title.

(H. Wheeler Robinson, *The Religious Ideas of the OT*, 198ff; Vincent Taylor, *The Names of Jesus*, 18ff)

DIABOLOS—SATAN, THE DEVIL

From *diaballein*, to throw over, e.g. in wrestling. Hence to attack a man's character, sometimes by just accusation, more often slanderously; to calumniate (Herodotus, Thucydides). In LXX for Satan.

THE OLD TESTAMENT
Heb. *Satan*.

1 Originally an adversary in the ordinary sense, e.g. of Hadad, Solomon's enemy (1 Kgs. 11:14).

2 In the Prologue to Job (Job 1:6ff; 2:1ff), the title of an official of the heavenly court, one of the "sons of God", whose function is to test the reality of men's piety. The Satan is very much subject to God, and cannot act without His leave.

3 In Zech. 3, the Satan is still man's accuser before God, but is rebuked for having accused Joshua falsely.

4 In 1 Chr. 21:1, Satan has become a proper name for the being who led David to number the people contrary to God's will; cf. the earlier 2 Sam. 24:1, where the enticement is attributed to God Himself. Here we have an example of dualism (probably due to Persian influence) in post-Exilic writing. The idea is that as God cannot be the originator of evil, it must therefore be attributable to another being.

5 In Wisdom of Solomon (written in Gk.), sin enters the world through the enmity of the Devil (*diabolos*)—Wisd. 2:24. Thus the Devil is identified with the serpent of Gen. 3 (cf. Rev. 12:9; 20:2).

THE NEW TESTAMENT
Satan or *diabolos*, also called "the evil one" (Mt. 5:37; 1 Jn. 2:13; 2 Thess. 3:3 (RV)), *Beelzebub* (Mt. 10:25), *Belial* (2 Cor. 6:15), *Apollyon* (=the Destroyer: Rev. 9:11).

1 The tempter of Jesus (Mt. 4; Lk. 4).

2 The enemy who enters into men and leads them into evil actions (Lk. 22:3; Jn. 13:27; cf. Mk. 8:33; Acts 5:3). The "murderer" and "Lord of death" (Heb. 2:14; cf. Mt. 10:28; Jn. 8:44).

3 His power in the world is such that he can be described as its present ruler (Jn. 12:31; 14:30; 16:11; 2 Cor. 4:4) and even of "the powers of the air" (Eph. 2:2).

4 He disguises himself as "an angel of light" (2 Cor. 11:14), therefore the Christian must be vigilant and resolute (2 Cor. 2:11; Eph. 6:11f; Ja. 4:7; 1 Pet. 5:8f).

5 His servants are his "angels" (lit. "messengers"—Gk. *angeloi*)—Mt. 25:41, and evil spirits (Mt. 12:43; 1 Tim. 4:1; Rev. 16:14), and his "sons", men in Satan's thrall (Jn. 8:44; Acts 13:10).

6 In all Satan's temptations, the believer is assured of God's faithfulness (1 Cor. 10:13; Col. 1:13; 2 Pet. 2:9; cf. Lk. 22:31), and Satan's final destruction is sure (Rom. 16:20; 1 Cor. 15:25-28; Rev. 14:10; cf. Mt. 13:41f; Lk. 10:18). Satan may be the prince of evil, but he can never finally be the prince of God's world. His doom is already pronounced.

(N. H. Snaith, *The Jews from Cyrus to Herod*, 132ff)

DIKAIOSŪNĒ—RIGHTEOUSNESS

Righteousness, justice (Herodotus, Plato). The adjective, *dikaios* originally meant observant of custom, civilized (Herodotus). Homer uses it to mean pious. Later it meant equal, well-balanced (e.g. of an even-running chariot), hence fair, lawful, just.

THE OLD TESTAMENT

Heb. *tsedeq, tsedaqah.*

1 Rightness, justice (Lev. 19:15; 2 Sam. 22:21), where the idea is just reward for uprightness and purity. The ethical prophets stress moral integrity and roundly condemn a false piety unaccompanied by honesty and fair dealing (Is. 1:10–21; Ezek. 33:13f; Hos. 10:2f; Amos 8:5; Mic. 6:11).

2 God's righteousness is not strict justice: He does not reward men strictly according to their deserts (Deut. 9:5f; Ps. 103:6ff). His loving-kindness (*chesed*) is always dominant, and the righteousness he "pours down" is salvation, not justice (Is. 45:8). Deutero-Isaiah (Is. 40–55) indeed can equate righteousness with salvation (*yeshuah, yesha*)—e.g. 51:8; cf. 46:13; 51:6.

3 Thus the righteousness required of man is more than mere justice: so in Deuteronomy (e.g. 24:13), there is special concern for the poor and needy, so that, even at the human level, mercy and kindness must always temper justice.

THE NEW TESTAMENT

1 *Dikaios* and *dikaiosūnē* can mean simply just, justice, right conduct in the moral sense (Mt. 5:10, 20; Acts 17:31; 1 Jn. 3:10; Rev. 19:11)—rendering to each his due (Tit. 1:8; 1 Jn. 1:9), but also conformity to the Divine will, i.e. what is right in God's eyes (Mt. 5:6; Jn. 16:8). Thus righteousness when used of men comes to mean man's religious duty (Lk. 1:75; Acts 10:35).

2 When used of God, *dikaiosūnē* means "what is in conformity with His nature of love", and practically equals salvation (*sōtēria*)—cf. Rom. 3:21.

3 We cannot establish our own righteousness (Rom. 10:3; Phil. 3:9)—that would be self-righteousness! Rather, righteousness comes by trust in God; it is the "righteousness of faith" (Rom. 9:30; Gal. 5:5; Heb. 11:7), and is a gift (Rom. 5:17).

4 Though righteousness is not earned but imputed (Rom. 4:1ff), once a man is in a faith relationship, he who was the slave of sin becomes the slave of righteousness (Rom. 6:18). Righteousness is not the *ground* of our salvation (Rom. 5:7f), but its natural *consequence*. He who is saved must live as if he is! In both OT and NT righteousness comes to mean much the same as salvation. The reason is simple. Righteousness means what is fundamentally right, while salvation means soundness, and a man cannot be wholly sound until he is fully saved.

(N. H. Snaith, *The Distinctive Ideas of the OT* (1944), 72ff)

DIKAIOUN—TO JUSTIFY

To set right in the legal sense (Pindarus): to hold or deem right, hence to do a man justice, pass sentence (Thucydides): to chastise, punish (Herodotus, Plato). LXX, to pronounce or treat as righteous, to vindicate.

THE OLD TESTAMENT

The verb *tsadaq*=to make or declare right, to justify or vindicate, comes from the same Heb. root as the adjective "righteous", and he who is justified is deemed to be righteous.

1 Sometimes it is God who is to be justified (Job. 32:2; Ps. 51:4), but generally He is the subject of the verb: it is Yahweh who justifies men.

2 Men must justify only the innocent: to do otherwise is morally reprehensible, especially to do so for reward (Deut. 25:1; Pro. 17:15; Is. 5:23). When an upright man is condemned by his fellows, he takes comfort from the knowledge that God will finally justify him (Is. 50:8).

3 In God's justification of men, a contradiction arises: on the one hand, it is asserted that man can be justified only on the grounds of actual righteousness (Ex. 23:7; cf. Ps. 15); on the other hand, the spiritually minded recognize that no man ever is completely innocent (Job 25:4; Ps. 143:2)! The fact is, of course, that in strict justice no man can be justified, but then, God is not a judge meting out strict justice in accordance with the statutes, but a Sovereign exercising the prerogative of approval or disapproval, of life or death, over His subjects solely according to His will. His sovereign judgment is the only judgment that matters, and in fact His nature is such that He accepts "a broken and contrite heart" (Ps. 51:17), allows vicarious justification of sinners by His righteous servant (Is. 53:11), and generally exercises mercy rather than justice (Ps. 103:10f).

4   When God justifies a man, then, He acquits him not on the ground of the man's innocence, but of His own sovereign mercy and love. That is not to say that God will never punish: He will—but punishment will not fit the crime, but the sinner's state of impenitence.

THE NEW TESTAMENT

Like *tsadaq, dikaioun* means to declare righteous, pronounce or treat as innocent, not, like Latin *justificare* (wrongly used in Vulgate for *dikaioun*) "make righteous". *Dikaioun*, in fact, is not really an ethical word at all.

1   In the Gospels, of man justifying God, or His wisdom (Mt. 11:19; Lk. 7:29); of men seeking to justify themselves (Lk. 10:29; 16:15); of God justifying the publican on the ground of his contrition (Lk. 18:14).

2   The main use of the verb is, however, Pauline, and occurs especially frequently in Romans and Galatians, in the course of his refutation of orthodox Judaism, which maintains that God will vindicate only the righteous who have perfectly kept the Law. Against this, the Apostle sets his own experience (Rom. 7) that man cannot hope for justification in his own right, for righteousness is impossible when men are fast-bound in sin. If man is to be justified at all, it must clearly be by an act of God's grace, on the ground of faith in Christ, who died for man's redemption (Rom. 3:24ff; 1 Cor. 6:11; Gal. 2:16; Tit. 3:7). Justification is a "free gift" (Rom. 5:16, 18), and is not a future hope, but a present privilege: we *are* justified (Rom. 3:28), *have been* justified (Rom. 5:1, 9:NEB). Justification, which is related both to Christ's death (Rom. 3:25; 5:9) and to His Resurrection (Rom. 4:25), is appropriated by faith—i.e. by accepting Christ as Lord and unreservedly placing ourselves at His disposal. This means, of course, that God justifies the wicked (Rom. 4:5)—a monstrous idea so long as we think in legalistic terms! Paul is making the point that legalistic terms are irrelevant: God acquits the guilty, it is true, but the acquittal is no mere legal fiction. The knowledge that God has pardoned frees us from the guilt which hinders communion with God, and brings a sense of peace (Rom. 5:1) conducive to moral effort: justified, we endeavour to

become what God has said we already are, and the battle against sin is already part won. We see this process working out in the Gospels, where Jesus treats sinners as if they were the men and women they have it in them to become: cf. Zacchaeus (Lk. 19:1ff), treated by the Jews as a lost sinner, by Jesus as a potential saint. Cf. also Lk. 7:36ff.

3 James three times uses *dikaioun* (Ja. 2:21, 24, 25), always of justification "by works". This is not a flat contradiction of the classical Pauline doctrine of justification by faith outlined above, but only a terminological difference. For Paul, "faith" is active and works by love (Gal. 5:6), while "works" are legalistic efforts to establish our own (self) righteousness (Rom. 10:3). In James, by contrast, "faith" is merely intellectual assent to theological propositions, which even a devil might give (Ja. 2:19), while "works" are the practical expression of religious conviction (Ja. 2:18). Nor do Paul and James use the verb in precisely the same sense. In Paul, *dikaioun* represents God's *present* acceptance of the sinner at the moment of faith, while James seems to think of it as His *final judgment* on a man's life, which must, of course, take into account the practical outworkings of the believer's faith (cf. Mt. 25:31–46 and Rom. 2:6). When these considerations are weighed, the apparent contradiction between the two writers largely disappears.

(DIKAIOSŪNĒ—RIGHTEOUSNESS. Sanday and Headlam, *ICC Romans*, 36f; C. H. Dodd, *M.N.T.C. Romans*, 51ff)

DOULOS—SERVANT

Properly of a born slave (or one enslaved by conquest), without personal rights, belonging body and soul to his master, and entirely dependent on his goodwill—cf. RVm "bondservant". For a paid servant, Greeks used *pais* (boy), much as the French use *garçon*: cf. Mt. 8:6; Lk. 15:26; Ac. 4:25.

THE OLD TESTAMENT

Heb. *ebed*, worker, servant, free-born or slave: even when a slave, however, he may hold a position of trust and responsibility (Gen. 15:2; 24).

1 The worshippers of Yahweh are His servants (Ps. 19:11; 86:2; Dan. 3:26), Abraham (Gen. 26:24), Moses (Ex. 14:31), David (2 Sam. 3:18) and the temple priesthood (Num. 18:7; Ezr. 6:18; Neh. 11:3) especially so.

2 Often all Israelites are regarded as God's servants (1 Kgs. 8:23; Ps. 102:14; Is. 41:8), but sometimes the term is restricted to the *righteous* in Israel (Ps. 35:27; Is. 65:8–14).

3 In the "Servant Songs" of Isaiah (42:1–7; 49:1–6; 50:4–9; 52:13–53:12) the concept is narrowed down to the one righteous servant who, by his innocent suffering, shall save the people. He is the true *ebed Yahweh*, perfectly in tune with His redemptive purpose. In these passages, LXX rightly rendered *ebed* by *pais*, not *doulos*.

THE NEW TESTAMENT

1 In the ordinary sense, slave, servant (Mt. 8:9; Jn. 18:10, etc.), but its true significance is religious.

2 All men are the slaves (*douloi*) of God (Mt. 25:14ff; Lk. 12:37 and other parables), and owe Him their total service (Lk. 17:10). Nevertheless, the Lord who can justly demand all, is

pleased with little, and the faithful servant will share His joy (Mt. 25:21).

3 Unregenerate man, far from being the faithful servant of God, has sold himself into the bondage of sin (Rom. 6:16ff; 2 Pet. 2:19). In the grip of sin, and powerless to release himself, he is bought by Christ, at the cost of His death (1 Cor. 7:23).

4 Henceforth, he is a slave of Christ, belonging body and soul to Him. He has passed into a new service, but it is a service of freedom: he is a friend of Christ (Jn. 15:15). He is not even a free servant, but a son (Gal. 4:3-7; cf. Lk. 15:19, 24).

DOXA—GLORY

In early Gk. (Homer, Herodotus), expectation, judgment, opinion. Later, estimation in which one is held, i.e. repute (generally good repute), prestige, honour, glory. In LXX for visible brightness, splendour—e.g. the radiance of God's presence in the pillar of cloud and the Holy of Holies (Ex. 16:10; 40:34 etc.) Eng. derivative, *doxology*=an ascription of glory.

THE OLD TESTAMENT
Heb. *kabod*, weight (cf. 2 Cor. 4:17), substance (Gen. 45:13; Ps. 49:16), hence honour which true worth commands.

(A) *Of Men*
1 Earthly glory (wealth, prestige, magnificence) of men, kings, nations (Est. 5:11; Job 19:9; Is. 10:3; Hos. 9:11).
2 The true glory which God gives to men when they take their rightful place in creation and obey Him (Ps. 8:5; Zech. 2:5).

(B) *Of God*
1 The glory which veils His presence on the mountain (Ex. 24:16) and in the temple (1 Kgs. 8:11; Ezek. 43:4; Hag. 2:7).
2 The Divine radiance in the heavens (Ps. 19:1) and the earth (Num. 14:21).
3 Of the glory to be revealed in the Messianic age, when "all flesh shall see it together" (Is. 40:5; cf. Ps. 102:16).
4 The honour due to Him from men in worship, obedience, sacrifice, etc. (Jos. 7:19; 1 Chr. 16:29; cf. Ps. 29:2; Mal. 2:2).

THE NEW TESTAMENT
(A) *Of Men*
1 Material well-being, honour, magnificence (Mt. 4:8; Lk. 12:27).

2 The glory God will give through our redemption in Christ (Jn. 17:22; Rom. 2:10; 1 Cor. 2:7; 1 Thess. 2:12).

3 The glory men give to God through thankfulness and by making His honour the goal of all their actions (Rom. 15:6ff; 1 Cor. 10:31; cf. Acts 12:23).

(B) *Of God and Jesus Christ*

1 The Divine glory reflected in all creation (1 Cor. 15:40f).

2 This glory is brought to a focus in Christ, who is "the brightness of His glory" (Heb. 1:3; cf. Jn. 1:14), "the Lord of glory" (1 Cor. 2:8; Ja. 2:1). Cf. 2 Cor. 4:6; 3:13ff for contrast with transient reflected glory in face of Moses (Ex. 34:29).

3 The glory of Christ, seen at Transfiguration (Lk. 9:32), is manifest to believers in the miracles (Jn. 11:4, 40).

4 More especially, Christ's *doxa* is manifested in His death and Resurrection (Lk. 24:26; 1 Pet. 1:21)—indeed, "His glory" becomes almost synonymous with the Passion. After all, God's greatest glory is His love in redemption (Cf. Eph. 3:16ff).

EIRĒNĒ—PEACE

Used by classical writers (Homer, Euripides al) in negative sense, absence of war, it is also the name of the goddess of peace, from whom we get the girl's name, Irene. In LXX almost invariably for Heb. *shalom* (related to place name, Salem and Oriental greeting *salaam*)—a much more positive word.

THE OLD TESTAMENT

1 Sometimes *shalom* is used in Gk. sense, freedom from strife (Jos. 9:15; 1 Sam. 7:14; 1 Kgs. 2:5), but generally in a much wider sense—the complete harmony of body, soul and spirit which is essential to a truly happy life (Gen. 15:15; Is. 54:13; Jer. 33:6; cf. Gen. 43:27, where "Is your father well?" is lit. "Is there peace to?")

2 Messiah will be called "Prince of Peace" (Is. 9:6), and will inaugurate an age of peace for all creation (Is. 11:2-9—cf. Mic. 4:1-3; Is. 32:15ff).

3 But *shalom* is always conditional: as the gift of God (Num. 6:26), one of the covenant mercies (Is. 54:10; Ezek. 34:25; 37:26), it is conditional upon faith and righteousness (Ps. 72:3-7; 85:8-11; Is. 32:17).

4 It is therefore idle to say "Peace, peace; when there is no peace" (Jer. 6:14; cf. 2 Kgs. 9:22). There is perfect peace for the man whose mind is fixed on God (Is. 26:3), but no peace for the wicked (Is. 48:22).

5 The OT does not distinguish between inner and external peace: the latter follows on the former (Ps. 122:6f): when men are right, nations will be right, and the world at peace.

THE NEW TESTAMENT

1 NT doctrine owes more to Hebraic than Gk. ideas—cf. the Epistles, where the usual Gk. salutation *chairein* (hail!,

greeting!) is replaced by *charis kai eirēnē*—"grace and peace" (Rom. 1:7; Col. 1:2; Rev. 1:4).

2   Peace, both freedom from exterior foe, and the inner harmony which is based upon righteousness, is ushered in by the birth of John Baptist (Lk. 1:71, 79) and Jesus (Lk. 2:14, 29f).

3   During Christ's ministry, peace is associated with wholeness (or salvation), and is the result of personal faith (Mk. 5:34; Lk. 7:50; 8:48).

4   But Jesus brings no easy peace; His coming is a judgment, and the peace of the Kingdom comes only upon those worthy to receive it (Mt. 10:34; Lk. 19:38, 42; cf. Lk. 10:5f). This must be so because Peace is not man-made but God-given (Phil. 1:2) —and the peace comes through the sacrifice of Christ (Jn. 14:27ff; Lk. 24:36; Acts 10:36; Rom. 5:1; Col. 1:20—cf. Heb. 7:2; 13:20).

5   Peace freely received is to be freely given; *eirēnē* is a fruit of the spirit (Gal. 5:22), and the Christian, at peace with God, will naturally seek to be at peace with men (Rom. 14:19; Eph. 4:3; 2 Tim. 2:22; Heb. 12:14). The man of God is not only a man at peace; he is a man of peace, and shows it in all he says and does (cf. Mt. 5:9).

EKKLĒSIA—CHURCH

This word, though common enough in ancient Greek (Thucydides, Plato, Aristoteles), was never used in a religious sense: *ekklēsia* meant a political assembly, city council or parliament, and is used in that sense by the Town Clerk in Acts 19:39. The religious use of the word (which gives us the adjective "ecclesiastical") comes from LXX, where it translates Heb. *qahal*, rendered in AV sometimes by "congregation", sometimes by "assembly".

THE OLD TESTAMENT

The word "church" does not occur in EVV, but the idea of a people of God is very prominent indeed, and is generally expressed in Heb. by *qahal* or *edhah*.

1 *Edhah*, the older word (common before the Exile, but later almost replaced by *qahal*) comes from a root meaning "to appoint". *Edhah Yahweh* is God's people, Israel, appointed by Him (Lev. 8:4; Num. 8:9; Ps. 111:1). LXX usually rendered *edhah* by Gk. *sünagōgē* (our "synagogue").

2 *Qahal* (root meaning "to call") was in the earlier period used of a gathering of the people for administrative purposes (Num. 1:18) or a muster for war (Jud. 20:2). Generally, however, it means the actual meeting together of the people of God, e.g. at Horeb, to receive the Law (Deut. 5:22), at the dedication of Solomon's temple (1 Kgs. 8:14f), and at the solemn republishing of the Law by Ezra (Ezr. 10:12). Through influence of LXX, *ekklēsia* (representing *qahal*) came to mean the whole people of God, while *sünagōgē* (for *edhah*) had the narrower meaning of a local worshipping congregation and sometimes even (like our word "church") the building in which it met.

3 Two important ideas emerge: (i) The people of God are *appointed* and *called*: they are His people because *He* has

47

appointed and called them. (ii) They are heirs to the privileges (and responsibilities!) of the Covenant. The early Christians, who knew their OT, were never in any danger of thinking of the Church as a human institution.

4 Old Testament prophets (like NT writers) often represent the people of God figuratively as His bride (Hos. 2:19), His child (Hos. 11:1), His vineyard (Is. 5:1–7; Hos. 10:1) etc. The point is obvious: Like a good wife, the Church should give love and loyalty to her Lord; like a good child, she should be obedient; like a good vineyard, she should produce a rich harvest, a harvest of righteousness and good works.

THE NEW TESTAMENT

1 *General. Ekklēsia* retains the definite theological emphasis of its Heb. antecedent *qahal*, and denotes the *People of God*— the Israel of the New Covenant (Heb. 12:23f), foreshadowed in the OT (Jer. 31:31ff), inaugurated by the sacrifice of Christ (Eph. 5:25), and founded on the faith of believers (Mt. 16:17f). By contrast, *sünagōgē* (representing Heb. *edhah*, and in the early books of LXX synonymous with *ekklēsia*) is a meeting for Jewish worship or the building in which it is held (Lk. 7:5). Church and synagogue, so close in OT origin, are now sharply opposed.

2 *The Gospels. Ekklēsia* (in the sense "Christian church") occurs only at Mt. 16:18 (twice in Mt. 18:17 it means the local Jewish community—though vv. 15–20 may be a later addition), but the institution is referred to by Jesus under the figures *flock* (Mt. 26:31), *little flock* (Lk. 12:32), and the *vine* (Jn. 15). In both Mt. and Jn., the occasion is the betrayal night, on which He spoke of the New Covenant (Mt. 26:28=Mk. 14:24=Lk. 22:20; cf. 1 Cor. 11:25). Lk. 12:32 makes it clear that though the church must not be equated with the Kingdom, the members of the former are heirs of the latter.

3 *Acts and Epistles. Ekklēsia* is much commoner. First used of the little community of baptized, spirit-filled believers in Jerusalem (Acts 5:11), the word is soon used in two senses: in the singular of local churches in various cities (Acts 15:3; 18:22; 20:17) and private houses (1 Cor. 14:19; Col. 4:15), but also of the whole church (Acts 20:28; cf. Gal. 1:13, where persecution

48

of the Christians at Jerusalem is persecution of *the church of God*). The church is one, and even when the plural (*ekklēsiai*) is used (Gal. 1:2), the several churches are local manifestations of a single body; wherever worshipping believers are, there is the church, active and visible. The church is not "my" or "our" church: it is divinely instituted, a Messianic community inaugurated by the redemptive act of God in Christ—the *church of God* (1 Cor. 1:2), the *church of Christ* (Rom. 16:16), the "church of God in Christ" (1 Thess. 2:14). The relation of Christ to His church is clearly brought out in the metaphors used: *Body* (1 Cor. 12:12ff; Eph. 1:22; 5:23—Christ the *Head*: cf. Col. 1:18, 24), *Bride* (Eph. 5:23ff; cf. Rev. 21:2—Christ the *Bridegroom*), the *Temple* or *Spiritual House* (1 Cor. 3:16f; 2 Cor. 6:16; Eph. 2:20f—Christ the *Corner Stone*: 1 Pet. 2:5; 1 Tim. 3:15; cf. 1 Cor. 3:11—Christ the *Foundation*), the *Royal Priesthood* or *Holy Nation* (1 Pet. 2:5, 9). The church is the fellowship of believers, married to Christ, led by the Spirit, living a life of prayer and praise, and exercising His priestly ministry among men. The NT knows nothing of Christians who are not churchmen: such as are being saved naturally join Christ's church (Acts 2:47), and in its local fellowship find their place and their work.

(F. J. A. Hort, *The Christian Ecclesia*; R. N. Flew, *Jesus and His Church*)

ELEOS—MERCY

Homer, Plato al. use *eleos* of pity, mercy, compassion, and the word also occurs as the name of the god of clemency, worshipped at Athens and Epidaurus. In LXX, *eleos* is the ordinary word for mercy and generally translates Heb. *chesed*.

THE OLD TESTAMENT

1 *Chesed* is sometimes rendered *kindness* (Gen. 40:14; 2 Sam. 2:5; Is. 54:8; Joel 2:13; Jon. 4:2), but more often *mercy*. Sometimes it is kindness or mercy from man to man (Gen. 19:19; Hos. 6:6; Mic. 6:8), but usually God's mercy.

2 Because Yahweh has a passion for righteousness, His *chesed* is to them who keep covenant (Ex. 20:6; Deut. 7:9; Ps. 103:17; Is. 55:3): because He has an even more passionate love for His people, his *chesed* embraces also the faithless and the fallen (Lam. 3:22, 32; Mic. 7:18).

3 This word is often (especially in Psalms) rendered in EVV by Coverdale's coinage "lovingkindness"—Ps. 36:7; 63:3, etc. (23 times in all); also Is. 63:7; Jer. 9:24; 31:3; Hos. 2:19. In all these passages, RSV has the excellent translation "steadfast love". *Chesed* always has the overtones of loyalty to an agreement: it is the kindness or mercy properly exercised by those bound by solemn compact—cf. Jer. 2:2, where *chesed* (EVV "kindness") is immediately followed by "the love of thine espousals".

4 *Chesed*, then, expresses God's loyalty to the Covenant even when men prove faithless—His steadfast love which makes Him ever ready to forgive—and is, perhaps, the nearest approach in OT to the NT doctrine of grace.

5 Two other Heb. words are rendered "mercy" in EVV—*racham*, which denotes God's tender compassion for man's frailty (1 Chr. 21:13; Neh. 9:27; Is. 49:13) and *chanan* (mainly in Psalms), which speaks of God's kindly and generous dis-

position in protecting the weak (Ps. 56:1; 57:1 etc.). Neither word is so important as *chesed*.

1 *Eleos* is sometimes used of human mercy (Lk. 10:37; Ja. 2:13; 3:17), but more often denotes God's attitude to man— either His general forbearance, as in Magnificat (Lk. 1:50, 54— reminiscences of OT passages in which the Heb. word is *chesed*), or, more especially, His mercy in Christ Jesus—Rom. 15:9; Eph. 2:4; Tit. 3:5; Heb. 4:16; 1 Pet. 1:3.

2 Rom. 9:22f is particularly instructive; sinful man, properly an object of Divine wrath, fit only for destruction, becomes an object of Divine mercy, destined for glory. Here, and in the other passages which speak of God's mercy in Christ, *eleos* is not mere pity or clemency in its original Gk. sense, but the undeserved favour of God of which the prophets told—His loving-kindness towards a perverse and wayward humanity. God does not deal with us in justice, according to our sins, but in mercy, according to His love.

(N. H. Snaith, *The Distinctive Ideas of the OT*, Ch. V)

ELPIS—HOPE

Common in classical literature, where it is used generally of hope or expectation, usually good hope, rarely (e.g. Aeschylus, Hippocrates) of bad hope, foreboding. In NT *elpis* is invariably used in the good sense.

THE OLD TESTAMENT

The two main Heb. equivalents are *betach*—"confidence" (Ps. 16:9; the cognate verb, *batach* is generally rendered "trust" in EVV—2 Kgs. 18:5; Ps. 4:5; Is. 12:2; Jer. 17:7 etc.), and *tiqvah*—hope, expectation (Job 11:18; Ps. 71:5; Jer. 31:17 etc.).

1 The hope of the Israelite is always in God (Jer. 14:8), and trust in wealth (Job 31:24), military strength (Ps. 20:7), man (Jer. 17:5) or even righteousness (Ezek. 33:13) is vain.

2 Israel used to hope for a change of fortune in the New Year (cf. Jer. 8:20), but the good times never came. The prophets said the only real hope was in the Day of the Lord, when Messiah would establish his kingdom (Joel 3:16ff).

3 The kingdom would be a kingdom of righteousness, and the prophets warned that it would involve a sifting of Israel (Amos 5). The warning was not heeded, and the coming of Messiah found the people unprepared.

THE NEW TESTAMENT

1 OT hoped in "Him who should come": NT hopes in Him who came once in humility and will come again in glory. Our hope is based upon the mighty acts of God (Rom. 15:4), and especially on the Resurrection of Christ (1 Pet. 1:3).

2 Often contrary to human expectation (as the Resurrection was!) it is "hope against hope" (Rom. 4:18), but it is also certain because is rests on the promises of a faithful and changeless

God (Heb. 10:23), who has given us the Spirit as a first instalment (2 Cor. 1:22; 5:5; Eph. 1:14).

3 Thus, though our hope is eschatological (in that it is fully consummated only at the end of time, at the second coming), because Christ is now in us, the hope of glory (Col. 1:27), it is also a present reality, and we can say "by hope we *were* saved" (Rom. 8:24). We are sure of the future because of what Christ has done in the past, and because we know that He is with us in the present. Therefore our hope is steadfast and never lets us down (Rom. 5:5; 1 Thess. 1:3; Heb. 6:19). Hope, then, is not general optimism or pious dreaming, but a reasoning confidence in God's grace in the future based upon our experience of Him in the past.

4 Hope is closely linked with faith (*pistis*), because faith is the ground of our hope (Heb. 11:1), and hope (of life eternal) the object of faith (Tit. 1:1f). It is also linked with love (*agapē*) because Christian hope can never be selfish, but must always include the salvation of others (2 Cor. 1:7).

EUANGELION—GOSPEL

Our words evangelist, evangelical come from this Gk. noun, which originally (e.g. The Odyssey; cf. 2 Sam 4:10 (LXX)) meant a reward for bringing good news—the herald's wages. In Isocrates and Menander, *euangelia* (pl.) is used of a thank-offering for good tidings. Gradually it came to mean the actual good news brought—so Lucian and Plutarch. The cognate verb (*euangelizesthai*) is used in LXX at our 1 Sam. 31:9 of carrying news in general; in Ps. 40:10; 96:2 of declaring God's loving-kindness; in Is. 61:1 of the Messianic proclamation of deliverance. In NT, *euangelion* is always Christ's good news of the Kingdom of God, and the verb means "to preach the Gospel": for these, of course, there is no strict OT equivalent. The English word "gospel" comes from Anglo-Saxon *godspel*—"good tidings" or "God-story".

THE NEW TESTAMENT

1 Jesus refers the prophecy of Is. 61:1 to Himself (Lk. 4:18); His preaching and healing prove that Messiah has come, that the Kingdom is at hand. Now men must respond in repentance and faith (Mk. 1:15).

2 After the Resurrection, the Gospel is seen to be not just the proclamation of the Kingdom, but the good news of what God has done for man's redempion by the life, death and resurrection of His Son. It is therefore "the gospel of Christ" (Rom. 15:19) and "of God" (Rom. 15:16). No other gospel, whatever its source, will suffice (Gal. 1:6-9).

3 The Gospel is preached, but not all hear (Rom. 10:15f); it remains hidden (2 Cor. 4:3) and a mystery (Eph. 6:19) except to those who grasp it by faith—it is "the power of God unto salvation" only to them who believe. Salvation is the gift of God in Christ and, like all gifts, has to be received to be enjoyed.

4 Acceptance of the Gospel involves moral obligations: those

who are saved must show it by their lives (Eph. 4:1; Phil. 1:27; 1 Thess. 2:12).

5 The Gospel, once accepted, proves to be one of power (Rom. 1:16), grace (Acts 20:24), truth (Col. 1:5), and peace (Eph. 6:15).

6 Though the Gospel is "the Gospel of Christ", it is also "my" or "our" Gospel (Rom. 2:16; 2 Cor. 4:3, etc.), and only as we personally grasp it can we be effective in the service of Christ (Eph. 3:3ff).

7 *Euangelion* does not occur in the Johannine writings (except in Rev. 14:6f, where it is only a proclamation of judgment): the Gospel is there in good measure, of course, but the author prefers to describe it by the word *marturia*—witness, testimony.

8 *Euangelion* is never used in the sense of an account of the life and teaching of Jesus, as when we speak of "The Gospel according to Matthew" etc. That is a later usage, dating only from the second century.

HADĒS—HELL

In Homer, the name of the God of the Underworld (=Pluto). Later, of the place of departed spirits, hence "death", "the grave". In LXX, chiefly for *Sheol*.

THE OLD TESTAMENT

Heb. *Sheol* (AV sometimes "pit", generally "hell" or "the grave". RV "the grave", "the pit", and in poetical writings, "Sheol" (RVm "the grave"): only in Is. 14, "hell" (RVm. "Sheol"). RSV, always "Sheol".

1 Not a place of torture, but the underworld (Num. 16:30ff; Amos 9:2), where worms destroy the body (Is. 14:11), and good and bad alike lead an inactive and shadowy (but conscious) existence. *Sheol* is the great leveller: even the great ones of the earth must experience its weakness and futility (Job 3:11ff; Ps. 49:17; Is. 14:10). In *Sheol* man is cut off from all fellowship with God (Ps. 6:5; 88:4f, 10–12; Is. 38:18), and from *Sheol* there is no return (2 Sam. 12:23). True, there was a popular belief that the great dead, at least, could be temporarily raised by those with "a familiar spirit" (1 Sam. 28), but necromancy and spiritualism were fiercely condemned by the orthodox (Deut. 18:9ff; Is. 8:19).

2 Developing belief in Yahweh's universal sovereignty extended His sway to *Sheol* (i.e. the nethermost parts of the world) —e.g. Ps. 139:8, though here the writer is giving poetical expression to God's omnipresence rather than propounding a doctrine of the future life. AV of Job 19:25f seems to affirm a bodily resurrection, but the Heb. text merely envisages *earthly* vindication after disease has stripped off the skin from the Prophet's body—not disembodied existence after death, which would be unthinkable to a Hebrew (cf. 1 Cor. 15:35ff). Nor is there any doctrine of immortality in two passages from Psalms sometimes

taken in EVV to imply a future life. Ps. 73:24: "afterward thou wilt receive me to glory (*kabod*)", seems to look only for earthly prosperity and honour after the writer's present troubles have ceased—it is unlikely that *kabod* means heavenly glory. The other, Ps. 49:15: "God will ransom my soul from Sheol", which at first glance appears promising, is set in the context of man's inescapable finitude and mortality.

3 Only two very late passages, Is. 26:19 and Dan. 12:2, speak clearly of life after death: the former affirms that the righteous dead shall rise to share the coming deliverance, the latter teaches a resurrection of the righteous dead to everlasting life, the unrighteous to everlasting shame. Both passages are apocalyptic, and indeed it was the despair of ever redressing on earth the injustices suffered by the godly, and the consequent growth of the apocalyptic expectation of the Day of the Lord in which God would set things to rights, which led to belief in resurrection and individual retribution after death. In the apocryphal literature, these ideas are elaborated: sometimes (e.g. Wisd. 3:5; Enoch; Ps. of Solomon) it is only the righteous who rise to share the blessings of the New Age; sometimes (e.g. 2 Esd. 7:32–36) there is more general retribution—bliss for the righteous, torment for the wicked.

4 By NT times, the Scribes and Pharisees and the popular synagogue religion which they represented fully accepted resurrection and future life, though their doctrines were not at all clear-cut. The priestly Sadducees (representing the more conservative Temple religion) denied both (cf. Acts 23:6–8) because they could not be proved from the Pentateuch—hence the point of Jesus' argument, Mt. 22:29ff. Some belief in a life hereafter was almost universal, then, in the Judaism of Jesus' day, but only His own Resurrection gave it real form and substance.

(OURANOS—HEAVEN. J. N. Schofield, *Archaeology and the After-Life*)

THE NEW TESTAMENT

Two words are rendered "hell" in AV—*Hadēs* and *Geenna*.

I. HADĒS (RV "Hadēs", RSV "Hadēs", except in Mt. 16:18: "death").

1 The abode of the dead in the centre of the earth (Mt. 12:40), a prison (1 Pet. 3:19; cf. Rev. 20:2, 7) with locked gates (Mt. 16:18) of which Christ has the keys (Rev. 1:18).

2 Except for Lk. 16:23 (and here it may be purgatory rather than hell), not a place of torture but the place in which the dead await the final resurrection at the return of Christ (Rev. 6:9ff; 20:13).

3. The descent of Jesus into *Hadēs* (1 Pet. 3:19) both underlines the completeness of His experience of death and His universal sovereignty (so that even in *Hadēs* men cannot be separated from Him—cf. Rom. 8:38ff), and asserts that the offer of the Gospel was made to those already dead. Whether this implies a further chance of salvation for all men, even those who rejected it in life (and Lk. 16:31 may throw doubt on this) or a once only appeal to those (i.e. OT saints) who died before Christ's earthly ministry began, is open to question.

4 Mt. 16:18 is the guarantee that the Church extends both sides of the grave, the "communion of saints" (i.e. fellowship of believers), being unbroken by death (cf. "the Church militant on earth, triumphant in heaven").

II GEENNA (Hell proper)—a transliteration of Heb. *Ge Hinnom*, a valley S. of Jerusalem where Ahaz and Manasseh offered child sacrifice to Moloch (2 Chr. 28:3; 33:36; Jer. 32:35). The site was defiled by Josiah during the reformation in which he put down pagan worship (2 Kgs. 23:10). Later it became a garbage dump, and its burning fires made it a symbol of judgment (Jer. 7:31ff; 19:6ff; cf. Is. 66:24). In apocalyptic writings (1 Enoch 27; 90:26f) it is the place in which the wicked are punished in sight of the righteous.

1 *Geenna* mentioned rarely (Mt. 5:22, 29, 30; Mk. 9:43, 45, 47; Lk. 12:5; Ja. 3:6), almost always in words of Jesus.

2 It is a place of torment and unquenchable fire (Mt. 18:8f; Mk. 9:44ff), a furnace (Mt. 13:42), a lake of fire (Rev. 20:14), outer darkness (i.e. banishment from the Light of the World— cf. Jn. 13:30; Acts 1:25)—Mt. 8:12.

3 Elsewhere final punishment is expressed by "wrath" (Rom. 5:9), "destruction" (Rom. 9:22), "corruption" (Gal. 6:8), "death" (Jn. 8:21), "the second death" (Rev. 20:6, 14) etc.

4   While fiery torment need not be taken literally, neither can the warnings of Christ be ignored. Hell is an integral part of His teaching, a necessary reminder of the dreadful fate which awaits those who finally reject the offer of salvation.

HAGIOS—HOLY

Devoted to the gods, sacred (Plato, Xenophon); of persons, holy, pure (Aristophanes). Not found in Homer, Hesiod or Tragedians.

Heb. *qadosh*, separate, set apart—that which is dedicated to the service of God, and therefore is not to be used for any ordinary purpose.

1 The sanctuary (Ex. 28:29) and various articles of priestly apparel (Ex. 29:6; Lev. 16:4; 1 Kgs. 8:4) are "holy" because they belong to God and are not for profane use.

2 As with things, so with men—e.g. Nazirites (Num. 6:5), Prophets (2 Kgs. 4:9; cf. Lk. 1:70) are dedicated to God and so "holy".

3 The distinction between the holy and that which is for common use is to be rigorously observed (Ezek. 44:23).

4 Because only the best can be fitly offered to God, *qadosh* gradually shaded over in meaning from "that which is God's own" to "that which is worthy of God"—i.e. *pure*. Thus sacrifices offered on the altar must be spotless (Lev. 22:17ff), the priests who officiate must be perfect specimens of manhood (Lev. 21:16ff).

5 Yahweh is the Holy One of Israel (2 Kgs. 19:22; Ps. 78:41; Jer. 50:29): He is holy in the sense that He stands completely above the created world, is the "wholly other" (Is. 40:25; cf. Job 4:17; 42:1–6; Hos. 11:9).

6 God is not only different from men—He is altogether superior to them in goodness (Deut. 32:4), and His perfection can find no place for sin (Hab. 1:13). Because God is what He is (Hos. 11:9), His nature (His holiness) will be shown in acts of mercy (Jer. 51:1) and redemption (Ps. 71:22f; Is. 43:3). He will

redeem men from evil that they may become like Him (cf. Heb. 12:10).

7 Israel belongs to God (that is what the Bible means when it says God "sanctifies His people"—Ezek. 37:28 etc.), therefore they are different from all other peoples. But they are also to be pure: God gives them His law and expects from them a higher moral standard than from the heathen (Ex. 19:6; Lev. 19:2ff; Ezek. 37:27ff; Hos. 2:23; cf. Jer. 31:18–20, 22, 31ff). When talking of God or men, holiness and righteousness can never be separated.

THE NEW TESTAMENT

Again the twin ideas of dedication and purity are found.

1 Jesus is called "holy" (Lk. 1:35; Rev. 3:7), "the holy one of God" (Lk. 4:34; Jn. 6:69), "thy holy servant Jesus" (Acts 4:27, 30), and "the holy and righteous one" (Acts 3:14). He is holy because completely dedicated to the service of the Father (Lk. 2:49; Jn. 9:4; 17:4), and therefore different from common men. The difference is manifest in His unique knowledge (Jn. 7:15f) and authority (Mt. 7:28; Jn. 7:47), in His power over disease and the forces of evil (Mk. 1:24; Lk. 4:36), power to forgive sin (Lk. 5:24) and to redeem (Gal. 3:13), and power over life and death (Lk. 10:19; Jn. 10:18). The purity of Jesus is seen in His complete freedom from sin (Jn. 8:46; Heb. 4:15) and His devotion to good works (Acts 10:38).

2 Christians are called *HOI HAGIOI* (pl.)—"the holy ones" or "saints" (Acts 9:13; Rom. 1:7; 1 Cor. 16:1; Eph. 5:3; Phil. 4:22; Ju. 3, etc.), and again both dedication and purity is implied. The disciple will inevitably reject the world's standards, and himself be scorned by men of the world (Mt. 5:10f; 10:25; Mk. 8:34; Lk. 16:13; Rom. 12:2). He will be different, not in a narrow, exclusive way—"holier than thou" (it is our righteousness, not self-righteousness, which is to exceed that of the Scribes and Pharisees!), but in the extent of his self-dedication. The believer is to "present his body (i.e. life) a living sacrifice, holy, acceptable to God" (Rom. 12:1): this, says Paul is our "reasonable service". In other words, holiness is not required only of a few specialists in religion: it is demanded by Christ of *all* who belong to Him.

3 If this demand seems excessive, we must remember how things come to be holy. The place of the burning bush is holy because God is there; the temple is holy because it is God's house; the prophet because he is God's man. All holiness is *derived*—things and people are holy only as they are near Him who is holy. Holiness is always *given*—it is given by grace and received through faith (Eph. 1:4; 3:16ff; Phil. 3:9, 12).

(N. H. Snaith, *The Distinctive Ideas of the OT*, 21ff; R. Otto, *The Idea of the Holy*, E. T. by J. W. Harvey)

HAMARTIA—SIN

Failure, fault (Aristotle), error of judgment (Thucydides), relig., guilt, sin (Plato). The cognate verb, *hamartanein*, means to miss the mark, fail in one's purpose, go astray.

THE OLD TESTAMENT

1 Among the many words used for sin (in our EVV rendered error, fault, iniquity, offence, transgression, etc.), three are of special importance: (i) *chattath* (Gen. 4:7; Lev. 16:30; 1 Kgs. 8:34; Is. 30:1; Amos 5:12, etc.), from a root meaning to err, stray, fail, miss the mark. Sin is error or failure; the sinner is on the wrong road. The righteous man is on the right road, loves God and walks in His ways (Deut. 30:16). (ii) *Awon*, iniquity, perversity (Gen. 19:15; 2 Sam. 19:19; Job 31:28; Ps. 18:23, etc.). God created man good (Gen. 1:27, 31); goodness is his normal state, sin is perversity, a terrible aberration which destroys his inner harmony. (iii) *Pesha*, trespass, transgression, rebellion (1 Kgs. 8:50; Job 7:21; Ps. 19:13; Amos 3:14, etc.). The sinner has set his face against God: sin is defiance of the Creator, downright rebellion.

2 Sin is never *simply* error or failure: the sinner is not a poor simpleton more to be pitied than blamed. There is always the element of perversity and rebellion to be reckoned with— the sinner is wrong-headed, a "fool" in the Biblical sense, one who trusts in himself (Prov. 28:26), acts as if there were no God (Ps. 14:1; 53:1) and therefore errs exceedingly (1 Sam. 26:21). The sinner is a fool more to be blamed than pitied.

3 Because sin is always a compound thing, the OT often links together two or more words the better to describe the extent of the malady—cf. Ps. 85:2 (*awon* and *chattath*); Job 34:37 (*pesha* and *chattath*); Ex. 34:7 (*awon* and *pesha*).

4 The consequences of sin are far-reaching: (i) it brings shame and guilt and destroys man's inner peace (Gen. 3:11; Is.

57:20, etc.). (ii) It leads to social strife, setting man against his fellows (Ps. 55:9–11), (iii) It provokes God to anger (1 Kgs. 16:13, etc.), and calls down punishment (Lev. 26:18; Amos 3:2, etc.).

Several words, *adikia*—unrighteousness, *anomia*—lawlessness, *hamartēma*—act of disobedience, *paraptōma*—trespass, are covered by the generic term *hamartia*—cf. 1 Jn. 3:4; 5:17.

1 *Synoptics.* The name Jesus means "the Lord will save" (cf. Mt. 1:21); John Baptist preached repentance unto remission of sins (Mk. 1:4). Repentance was involved in Jesus' proclamation of the Kingdom (Mk. 1:15), while the parables explain His Divine work as the saving of the lost, the crooked and the rebellious (Lk. 15; 19:10). Forgiveness is associated with cure in the healing miracles (Mt. 9:2ff; cf. Jn. 5:14)—this is in line with Hebrew thought and much modern psychology. Indeed Gk. verb *sōzein* can mean either "cure" (Mk. 5:34, etc.) or "save" (Mk. 10:26, etc.) The death of Jesus, like His life, is in the service of sinners (Mt. 20:28b). Jesus does not speculate on the *origin* of sin, but accepts the *fact*. He expressly denies that suffering falls only on the sinner (Lk. 13:2; cf. Jn. 9:2f).

2 *Johannine Writings. Hamartia* is a spiritual condition, the opposite of *alētheia* (truth)—Jn. 9:41; 15:24; 1 Jn. 1:8. It is wilful blindness to God's purpose, a *revolt* of the flesh (1 Jn. 2:16ff). In our natural state, we are all sinners, but those who are born of God and abide in Christ do not sin (1 Jn. 3:6; 5:18). Perfect love casts out sin as it casts out fear.

3 *Paul.* Sin is a personal power of evil ruling in the world (Eph. 6:12), dwelling in the flesh (Rom. 7:7, 20), enslaving *all* men, and making them impotent of good (Rom. 3:23; 6:6; 7:14ff). This thraldom ("original sin") is inherited from Adam, consequently man must serve sin and receive its deadly wages (Rom. 5:12; 6:23). Adam's disobedience involved men in death; Christ's obedience brings them life (1 Cor. 15:22). The emphasis is generally on the *condition* of sin, but Paul warns also against specific *sins* (1 Cor. 5:9–11; 6:9f; Eph. 5:5; 1 Tim. 6:4f) "for the unrighteous shall not inherit the kingdom of God".

4 *Hebrews.* Sin is a power which deceives men and lures them

to destruction (3:13). Its power can be broken only by Christ, the great High Priest who, because of His complete self-identification with men, can bear gently with the erring (5:1) and, because of His sinlessness, can offer the perfect sacrifice (9:14f) not repeatedly (as with OT sacrifice), but once for all (9:24ff).

HĒMERA—DAY

This word, which gives us the adjective *ephemeral*, was the ordinary word for daytime as opposed to night. *Hēmera* was also sometimes used in time of life, youth and age, and, in the poets, in the historical sense, "in the days of . . .", a usage familiar enough to us.

THE OLD TESTAMENT
Heb. *yom*

1 Literally, a day (Gen. 1:5), or light as opposed to darkness (Gen. 1:5).

2 Of longer periods—Num. 13:20: "Now the time (yom) was the time of the first ripe grapes"; Neh. 9:32: "Since the time of the kings of Assyria".

3 Of age; Zech. 8:4: "His staff in his hand for very age" (lit. "for multitude of days").

4 Most importantly, however, of the longed for Day of the Lord, when Yahweh would put down His enemies, redress the misfortunes of Israel, and bring in a time of prosperity and happiness for His people. Amos (5:18) warns that as God's enemy is unrighteousness, the wickedness of Israel will come under condemnation, and therefore the Day of the Lord will be darkness and not light! Zeph. 1:14ff enlarges on the calamities of that Day, while Is. 13:10ff; Joel 2:30ff; 3:2, 4, 12 fill in the lurid details. Here we see what is called *apocalyptic* taking shape and moving towards the idea of a Grand Assize at the end of the age —a time of reckoning between God and man. Alas! Israel largely ignored the prophetic warning that she would be judged for her sin and, especially after the Exile, the Day of the Lord was generally thought of nationalistically as a Day of Judgment on the heathen (e.g. Zech. 14:9ff). It is always easier to see others' sin than one's own!

1 *Hēmera* used in the ordinary sense (Mk. 4:35; Lk. 17:4, etc.).

2 In the sense of *times* (Mt. 2:1; Acts 5:37).

3 Of the Day of the Lord (1 Thess. 5:2; 2 Pet. 3:10) or "of Jesus Christ" (Phil. 1:6; 2 Thess. 2:2). This is a Day of Judgment (Mt. 12:36; Mk. 6:11; 2 Pet. 2:9f; cf. Mk. 13:14ff—"the little apocalypse"; Lk. 17:30f; Rom. 2:16), and impenitence stores up wrath for it (Rom. 2:5).

4 Although Jesus comes to preach a Gospel of grace, His coming both constitutes a judgment in itself (cf. Jn. 9:39), sorting men out in accordance with their response to Him, and also heralds a final judgment. When mercy has made its appeal, men must finally face their God and His Christ, to be judged according to their faith and the works that have flowed from it (Mt. 11:20ff; 25:31ff).

(N. H. Snaith, *The Jews From Cyrus to Herod*, 89f)

HIEREUS—PRIEST

Common in classical writers, inscriptions and papyri as the ordinary term for priests of the pagan religions—cf. Acts 14: 13. The NT word generally looks back to the OT, however; in several passages (Mt. 8:4, Lk. 10:31; Heb. 8:4, etc.), *hiereus* means simply "Jewish priest", but even where it does not, the idea behind the word is Hebraic rather than pagan.

THE OLD TESTAMENT

Heb. *kohen*, from which comes the common Jewish surname, Cohen.

1 The priest is an intermediary between man and God (Ex. 19:21f); he is a sacred person, belonging to God, and wears a badge "holy to the Lord" (Ex. 28:36). Because he must be fit to stand before God, he must be a perfect specimen of manhood (Lev. 21:17), must not shave (Lev. 21:5) and must avoid defilement (Lev. 21:1).

2 Priests used the *urim* and *thummim* (sacred dice carried in an apron, the *ephod*: 1 Sam. 28:6; Ezr. 2:63; 1 Sam. 23:9) to give decisions (called *tora*, pl. *toroth*) to those who enquired the will of God. They also carried out public health duties, medical inspection of lepers etc. (Lev. 14:2ff), and, as the literary class, were custodians of the Law; to them we owe successive editings of the Scriptures (cf. 2 Chr. 34:14ff).

3 In early times, laymen could offer sacrifice (Gideon, Manoah, Jud. 6:26; 13:19); later this became the exclusive prerogative and main function of the priests, and preservation and interpretation of the Law was delegated to the scribes.

4 In early times again, anybody might be consecrated priest (Micah's son (Jud. 17:5); David's sons (2 Sam. 8:18)), but later the priesthood was restricted to members of the tribe of Levi descended through Aaron. Non-Aaronite sons of Levi became Levites, a minor order of clergy.

5 After the Exile, the High Priest came into prominence as the head of the priesthood, and he it was who performed the rites of the Day of Atonement.

THE NEW TESTAMENT goes back behind the elaborate priesthood of later Judaism to the simplicity of ancient Israel.

1 *Hiereus*, used of individuals, means a Jewish (Acts 6:7) or pagan (Acts 14:13) priest, never an official of the Christian Church. True, our word "priest" comes from Gk. *presbüteros*, but this is due to later Church usage. *Presbüteros* means "elder" (in LXX "ambassador"), never "priest".

2 The word is used, however, (i) of Christ Himself, the only true High Priest, our only true Mediator (Heb. 5:6—quote from LXX); 7:3, 11; 10:21—see THUSIA—SACRIFICE). (ii) In pl. of all Christians in general—Rev. 1:6; 5:10; 20:6; cf. 1 Pet. 2:5, 9, where the word is *hierateuma*=priesthood.

3 In NT, then, we have one High Priest, Christ, through whom alone we have access to the Father (Jn. 14:6), and a vast company of ordinary priests, the members of His Church, who present their lives a spiritual sacrifice, and who are the ambassadors through whom God makes His appeal to men (Rom. 12:1; 2 Cor. 5:20). That is what the doctrine of the Priesthood of all Believers means, and it implies that as we are all priests, so we must all strive to be fit to stand before God.

(V. Parkin, *Priests in the Church of God*; T. F. Torrance, *Royal Priesthood*; A. C. Welch, *Prophet and Priest in Old Israel*)

ISRAEL

A transliteration of the new Heb. name given to Jacob at Peniel (Gen. 32:28). The most likely derivation is from *el* (God) and *sarar* (to reign), which would give the meaning "God strives" or "God rules".

THE OLD TESTAMENT

1 As a personal name=Jacob: Gen. 35:21; 1 Kgs. 18:36; etc.

2 Collectively, of his descendants, "Israel", "children of Israel", "sons of Israel", "my (thy) people Israel", etc. (i) In early times, of the twelve tribes, whose common bond was their worship of Yahweh (Ex. 1:9; Jos. 4:12; Jud. 5:2, 7–11; cf. Jos. 24). (ii) With the advent of the monarchy, *Israel* is used in a national or even geographical sense. The first king, Saul, failed to unite all twelve tribes (1 Sam. 11:8), and David at first ruled only Judah (2 Sam. 2:1–4, 8–11), though later he became king of Israel as well (2 Sam. 5:5). Solomon ruled the united kingdom, but at his death, the ten Northern tribes rebelled against Rehoboam and formed the independent kingdom of Israel, which continued its separate existence until it was overwhelmed by the Assyrian invasion of 722 BC. Davidic kings continued to rule the tiny Southern kingdom of Judah until it was overthrown by Babylon in 586 BC. (iii) After 722, when the political kingdom of Israel had disappeared, the name *Israel* regained its religious sense as the remnant of God's chosen people, all that remained of the people of God—i.e. the inhabitants of Judah! (So Is. 5:7; Jer. 2:4; 10:1; Mic. 3:1). By contrast, *Judah* was never used in this spiritual sense—it always remained a national or political name. The religious entity was *Israel*. (iv) After the Exile, *Judean* and *Jew* became the racial or national terms, and *Israel* developed an ideal (present or future) significance as the covenant people, the heirs of the promises, the religious community centred upon the

rebuilt temple (Is. 66:8ff; Ezek. 37:21ff; 47:21–48:7). This re-gathering of the dispersed members of Israel and Judah into a true and complete kingdom of David became increasingly the heart of Messianic expectation—cf. Acts. 1:6. But the prophets looked, too, to the restored *Israel* as the instrument of mission for the ingathering of the nations (Is. 44:1–5; Jonah), and this the Jews, absorbed in their imperialist dreams, largely forgot!

THE NEW TESTAMENT

1 The Patriarch Jacob (Rom. 9:6b), and especially his des-cendants, "the house of Israel" (Mt. 10:6; Acts 2:36; Heb. 8:10, etc.), "the sons of Israel" (Mt. 27:9; Lk. 1:16; Acts 5:21; Rom. 9:27b), or simply "Israel" (Lk. 2:25; Jn. 3:10).

2 The nation (Mt. 2:6; Lk. 1:54), its king (Mt. 27:42; Jn. 1:49; 12:13), its tribes (Mt. 19:28; Lk. 22:30; Rev. 7:4, etc.). *Israel* was the name Jews used of themselves (as it is now), but Gentiles called them *Ioudaioi* (sing. *Ioudaios*). *Ioudaios* is often used, too, in NT, especially by the Fourth Evangelist, who prefers it to *Israel*, and also in Acts (13:50; 17:5, etc.) of Jewish opponents of the Church. But *Ioudaios* has a racial or nationalist flavour: when the people of God is meant, NT generally prefers *Israel*. It is never the Israel of God which is in conflict with Jesus, but only those Jews who have forfeited all spiritual claim to belong to the elect (cf. Rom. 9:6).

3 Figuratively of Christians as the "true" or "divine" Israel (Gal. 6:16), the People of the New Covenant, the spiritual Israel as opposed to the physical (1 Cor. 10:18). Christ was to be Saviour of Israel (Mt. 2:6; Lk. 1:33; 2:34), therefore those whom He redeemed are Israel. We are the elect of God, and that is a great privilege. It is also a great responsibility, for we are to be God's agents in the calling of all the nations (2 Cor. 5:20; cf. Rom. 11:25).

4 Jews as such are not, of course, excluded from the new people of God; the miracles of Jesus were signs to Israel (Mt. 9:33), His first mission was restricted to them (Mt. 10:5ff; cf. 15:24) and many of the first converts were Jews (Acts 14:1). Paul describes himself as a Hebrew of Hebrews (Rom. 11:1; 2 Cor. 11:22; Phil. 3:5), but he is also of the true Israel which glories in Christ Jesus (Phil. 3:3), and that is the important thing!

Partitions may be broken down (Eph. 2:14), but just as in Christ the Law is not destroyed but fulfilled, so Israel is not done away but realized. There is not "no more Israel", but "no more Jew" (Gal. 3:28ff). *Israel* is not abolished by Christ, but enlarged by His calling of the Gentiles (Eph. 2:9ff; cf. Rom. 11). Israel remains, but it is a *New Israel* (the phrase is not in NT, though the idea is prominent enough), supranational, multiracial—the people over whom God reigns, the community of those who belong heart and soul to God, whatever their racial origin may be. The word has come full circle, back to its original meaning, only the conception of God's people is wider now, as the scope of the New Covenant is wider than the Old.

KARDIA—HEART

Classical writers use the word of the seat of emotion—rage, anger, fear, sorrow, etc., and of desire or purpose (i.e. mind). The medical writers Hippocrates and Galen use it in the physiological sense, from which we get the adjective cardiac. Like its Eng. equivalent, *kardia* was also used metaphorically of the centre of things—e.g. the pith of wood, the depths of the sea.

THE OLD TESTAMENT

Heb. *leb, lebab,* while used figuratively, "midst" (Deut. 4:11; 2 Sam. 18:14; Jon. 2:3, etc.), generally means the central driving force of a man, which regulates his spirit (*ruach*) and enables his *nephesh* (soul) to function properly.

1   The organ of thought (Gen. 6:5; Deut. 4:39; Is. 10:7), so sometimes rendered in EVV "mind" (Num. 24:13; Neh. 4:6; Ps. 31:12; Lam. 3:21). Thus to "steal a man's heart" (Gen. 31:20; 2 Sam. 15:6) is to hoodwink or fool him.

2   Of a whole range of emotional states—pride (Ob. 3; cf. Lk. 1:51), joy and sorrow (Jud. 18:20; 1 Sam. 1:8), anxiety and fear (1 Sam. 4:13; Gen. 42:28), courage (2 Sam. 17:10), love (2 Sam. 14:1), even drunkenness! (1 Sam. 25:36).

3   Of mental activities, memory (Deut. 4:9), understanding (1 Kgs. 3:9), technical skill (Ex. 28:3).

4   Of will and purpose (1 Sam. 2:35). The functions of the heart are as central as its anatomical position, and determine a man's disposition and character (2 Kgs. 10:15). God, who sees the heart of man (1 Sam. 16:7), knows it to be deceitful and wicked (Jer. 17:9), and since a wayward heart can only lead to perverse behaviour, God must give man a new heart (Jer. 24:7; Ezek. 11:19; 36:26). In a change of heart lies man's only hope.

THE NEW TESTAMENT

1   The centre and source of physical life (Acts 14:17; Ja. 5:5).

2   The faculty of thought and understanding, the organ of natural and spiritual enlightenment (2 Cor. 4:6; Eph. 1:18; 2 Pet. 1:19; cf. esp. Mt. 5:8). NEB rightly translates *kardia* by "mind" in several places—e.g. Rom. 1:21; 2 Cor. 3:15; 2 Pet. 1:19. As *kardia* is the seat of thought, so it is of doubt. (Mk. 11:23).

3   Will—2 Cor. 9:7: "as he has decided" (NEB); Lk. 21:14: "make up your minds" (NEB: Moff. "resolve").

4   The moral life, of virtues and vices (Mt. 5:28; Heb. 10:22; 2 Pet. 2:14).

5   Emotions and desires (Rom. 1:24; 2 Cor. 2:4; I Jn. 3:20—here *kardia*="conscience" (NEB)), especially of affection (Mk. 12:30; 2 Cor. 7:3; Phil. 1:7).

6   Disposition (Mt. 11:29; Acts 4:32; Eph. 6:5)—as his heart is, so, for better or worse, is the man (Mt. 12:34; 15:18; Lk. 6:45).

KĒRŪGMA—THE GOSPEL OUTLINE

Originally the reward offered by the town-crier in his proclamation (Xenophon); later it came to mean simply the message being proclaimed. In LXX, *kērügma* means a proclamation (e.g. of a royal edict—1 Ch. 30:5, or the preaching of a prophet (Jon. 3:2)).

Kērügma is rendered PREACHING (Mt. 12:41=Lk. 11:32; Rom. 16:25; 1 Cor. 1:21; 2:4 etc.), but true to its classical meaning, it is always the *content* rather than the act of preaching. It is the good news proclaimed in the apostolic preaching, the *essence* of the Gospel, and NEB well preserves the sense of 1 Cor. 15:14 when it renders simply "gospel".

1 Just as the town-crier is merely a mouth-piece, so the preacher is but the herald; his word is no human affair, but a proclamation from God, carrying all the authority of the King of Kings. The preacher is nothing, his message everything (cf. Rom. 1:15f; 1 Cor. 9:16; Gal. 1:7ff; Phil. 1:18ff; 2 Tim. 4:2ff).

2 Preaching is not the same as teaching; preaching is proclamation to the unconverted, teaching (*didachē*) is instruction given to those who already profess some faith—note the careful distinction in Mt. 4:23; 9:35. For the Apostles, *kērügma* was the evangelical message to the outsider; necessary instruction in Christian ethics, etc. to enquirers and catechumens was *didachē*. The distinction is a real one: the Sermon on the Mount is *didachē*, Peter's sermon in Acts 2, *kērügma*.

3 The *kērügma*, or outline of the gospel, which can be traced in the apostolic preaching, was fairly constant in form, and contained six elements: (i) Prophecy is fulfilled, and the latter days have come to pass (Acts 2:16; 3:18, 24). (ii) The fulfilment is in the life, death and resurrection of Jesus of Nazareth, whose

Messiahship is proved from the Scriptures. (iii) Through the Resurrection, Jesus has been exalted to God's right hand as Messianic leader of the New Israel (Acts 2:33–36; 3:13; 4:11). Scriptural proofs are again invoked. (iv) The Holy Spirit in the Church is the sign of Christ's present power and glory (Acts 2:33; 17–21; cf. Joel 2:28–32; Acts 5:32). (v) Christ will shortly come again to consummate the Messianic Age (Acts 3:21). (vi) An appeal for repentance, coupled with the offer of forgiveness and the gift of the Holy Spirit (Acts 2:38). The *kērügma*, then, is the Gospel in a nutshell—the bare bones of a Christian theology upon which the Apostles based their evangelical appeal, and which, nineteen centuries later, still represents the essence of the Faith. Modern scholars now use *KERYGMA* (u in Gk. has a "y" sound and can be so transliterated) as the technical term for this primitive Gospel-outline, which was later amplified into standard Christian formularies such as the Apostles' and Nicene Creeds.

(EUANGELION—GOSPEL. For the classical account of the *kērygma*, see C. H. Dodd, *The Apostolic Preaching*)

KOSMOS—WORLD

Either "order" or "adornment, ornament" (especially of women's finery—cf. 1 Pet. 3:3; "adorning": Homer uses the word in both senses. Pythagoras and Plato used it of the universe as an ordered system, and late writers simply of the earth, the world. Our derivatives, *cosmic, cosmetic* reflect the two Gk. usages.

THE OLD TESTAMENT

Tebel, "the habitable earth", "the world" (1 Sam. 2:8; Job 34:13; Ps. 50:12; 90:2; 98:7; Is. 27:6; Jer. 10:12) is probably the nearest Heb. equivalent, but several other words describe the world or its parts: *erets*—land, earth (Gen. 2:1; Deut. 4:18, etc.); *shamayim*—heaven (Gen. 1:1; Ex. 31:17; Jos. 2:11, etc.); etc.

1 For "world", Heb. often preferred "the heaven and the earth". There is, strictly, no OT theory of the universe, but collation of Gen. 1 with several other passages gives us a picture of the Heb. world-view. Like other nations round about, the Hebrews thought of a three-decker universe, with earth the middle storey. There was water above the vault of heaven (showering down as rain), and under the earth, from whence it bubbled up as springs. Gen. 11:4; 28:10–15 suggest that the heavenly vault was relatively low.

2 The place of departed spirits (*sheol*), was a vast cavern, deep in the earth, in which the dead had a shadowy existence (1 Sam. 28:14; Is. 14:9; Ezek. 32:17–32).

3 Though traces remain of early pagan creation myths, involving a primeval monster (*Rahab*: Job 9:13; 26:12; Ps. 74:13; Is. 51:9), they have been freed from polytheism: the hero is always Yahweh, the one true God and Creator—cf. Ps. 95:4, 5. God made the world from nothing, and the world is His, never man's.

4 Because God was Maker, the world is essentially good (Gen. 1:31), and evil in the world is man's doing (Gen. 3:17ff).

1 The world (i.e. the Earth—Mt. 4:8; Col. 2:20; 1 Tim 6:7).

2 Humanity (Mt. 5:14; 13:38; Jn. 1:10 (senses 1 and 2); Rom. 3:6; 2 Pet. 2:5, etc.).

3 Worldly affairs, material possessions (Mt. 16:26; 1 Cor. 7:31; 1 Jn. 2:16, etc.).

4 The ungodly, the world apart from God, worldliness (Jn. 7:7; 14:17; 1 Cor. 1:21; Ja. 1:27, etc.), and so:

5 The fallen world, ruled by Satan, and at enmity with God (Jn. 12:31; 16:11; 1 Cor. 2:12; 1 Jn. 5:19).

6 The fallen world is not, however, hopeless; God loves the world and will save it (Jn. 3:16; 4:42; 2 Cor. 5:19; Rev. 11:15). Most great world religions see matter as evil; Christianity views the world as essentially good, and offers cosmic salvation.

KRISIS—JUDGMENT

Our *crisis* derives from this classical word, which always signifies a decision or judgment, or the trial (of guilt in a law court (Antipho) or skill in an archery contest etc. (Sophocles)) which precedes it. In the Bible, *krisis* and its Heb. equivalents are generally used of God's judgment.

THE OLD TESTAMENT

There are two Heb. words, *mishpat* (judgment) and *din* (strict justice), the latter in later writings only. The corresponding verbs, *shaphat* and *din*, both mean to judge.

1 *Mishpat* is used (i) of the judgment according to precedent given at the local shrine—i.e. when the same question had been decided before. Where there is no precedent, and the priest must determine God's will by sacrifice or the casting of lots (or the prophet by ecstatic vision), the decision is called *torah*—instruction. As both *torah* and *mishpat* represent God's will, they gradually become synonymous with Law. Thus God's judgments are His commandments (Lev. 18:5; Deut. 26:17; Ps. 36:6; freq. in Ps. 119) (ii) By metonymy, of right judgment, righteousness (Is. 5:7; 59:11; Ho. 12:6; Am. 5:24 etc.) (iii) Of decisions given by prophets and kings in disputes of the people (Ju. 4:5; 2 Sam. 15:2 etc.).

2 Both *shaphat* and *din* are predicated of God not only as supreme Judge of Israel, but of the whole world (Gen. 18:25; 1 Chr. 16:33; Ps. 94:2, etc.); from Him all earthly magisterial power derives (2 Chr. 19:6). The judgment of Yahweh is demonstrated in all His saving acts in the crises of Heb. history (Jud. 2:16), and supremely in the Messianic judgment on the Day of the Lord (Is. 24–26).

THE NEW TESTAMENT

1 The standard of judgment, justice, righteousness (Mt. 12:18; 23:23; Jn. 7:24; 16:8).

2 An adverse judgment, condemnation (Ja. 5:12) or the punishment which follows (Mt. 23:33; Heb. 10:27; Ju. 15; Rev. 18:10).

3 Generally, however, *krisis* signifies God's judgment in Christ on human sinfulness. Jesus' ministry is a judgment—not that He condemns, but that men, by their rejection of Him, condemn themselves! (Jn. 3:17ff; cf. 9:39). The death of Christ is a judgment pronounced already on the world and the Devil (Jn. 12:31; 16:11). But this is not the final judgment, which will be pronounced on the Day of Judgment (Mt. 11:22; 13:36ff; 2 Pet. 2:9; cf. Ju. 6), when men will be judged according to the practical outworkings of their faith (Mt. 25 and other parables of the Kingdom).

4 Whether men are to be judged individually at death or all together at a Grand Assize at the end of the age (Lk. 16:22f; Heb. 9:27 *versus* Mt. 10:15; 12:42; 2 Pet. 2:4, 9) is not clear, and on a proper view of eternity (*timelessness*, not time of infinite duration) does not matter. What does matter is that we must all stand before the judgment seat of Christ. On that, the Gospel is very clear indeed (Rom. 14:10; 2 Cor. 5:10, etc.).

(HĒMERA—DAY)

KŪRIOS—LORD

In classical writers, *kūrios* always meant "one in authority", the head of a family, the master of a house, etc. In the vocative (*kūrie*), it was a respectful address—"sir", "milord". In Hellenistic times, *kūrios* was a title applied to Roman Emperors, subject kings (Herod the Gt., Agrippa al.), and the gods of mystery religions, Serapis, Isis.

THE OLD TESTAMENT

1 Heb. *adon* means ruler, master (Gen. 40:1; 45:8f). It is also used as a title of respect or courtesy (Gen. 42:10; Ru. 2:13; 1 Sam. 1:15).

2 The form *adonai*—lord, (i) When speaking to or of God (Gen. 15:2; Deut. 9:26; Ps. 37:13; Is. 4:4—about 130 times in all). (ii) In later Israel, from motives of reverence, God's name, Yahweh, was never spoken except by the High Priest; whenever the Name occured in scripture, the reader substituted *adonai*, which became, in effect, the Divine name. LXX followed this practice, translating Yahweh by *Kūrios*, and EVV by LORD in small caps. In the OT, then, Lord meant God the Creator, the Almighty.

THE NEW TESTAMENT

1 The master of a house or slave (Mk. 13:35; Acts 16:16). To designate a person of higher position—of husband in contrast to wife (1 Pet. 3:6), of the Emperor (Acts 25:26), as a respectful address from son to father (Mt. 21:30) or to a stranger (Jn. 12:21; Acts 16:30).

2 Of God, THE LORD (Mt. 5:33; Mk. 13:20; Acts 5:19; 2 Pet. 3:8; Rev. 11:15).

3 Jesus is called *Ho Kūrios*—the Lord, but probably not during His ministry; it is the risen and ascended Christ who is

Lord. True, the title occurs quite early in the Gospel story (Mt. 21:3; Lk. 1:43; 7, 13, 19, etc.), but as the Gospels were all written after the Ascension, these verses probably represent what had by then become common Christian usage. In Acts "the Lord Jesus" and "the (our) Lord Jesus Christ" are common (1:21; 8:16; 11:17; 20:21) and "the Lord" occurs about 20 times. Pauline and Catholic Epistles all speak of Jesus as "Lord", and Rom. 10:9; 1 Cor. 12:3 suggest that "Jesus is Lord" was the earliest Christian creed: the first Christians are "those who call upon the name of our Lord Jesus Christ" (1 Cor. 1:2; cf. Acts 9:14, etc.). Jesus was hailed as Lord not in Gk. only, but also in Aramaic—*Marana tha* —"Our Lord, come!", which shows that the usage is primitive.

4 To call Jesus *Kürios* implies two things (i) He is Master and Ruler to command, we are His *douloi* (slaves) to obey. (ii) He is truly Divine, God of Gods and Lord of Lords (Rev. 19:16)—not a good man to admire, but the Deity to worship and serve!

(O. Cullmann, *The Earliest Christian Confessions*; V. Taylor, *The Names of Jesus*)

LOGOS—WORD

Common in prose and verse at every stage in Gk. literature, *logos* has a great breadth of meaning—word, thing, account, reckoning, argument, explanation, oracle, rule, law, etc. In the Hellenistic world, it was a common philosophical term—see below, NT (4). *Logos* forms the termination -logy in such words as anthropology, geology, etc.

THE OLD TESTAMENT
Heb. *dabar.*

1 Question (1 Kgs. 10:3), matter, thing (Ex. 1:18; Est. 3:1), promise (Neh. 5:12), commandment (Ex. 34:28; Ps. 103:20), etc. It is not merely verbal: the Heb. mind did not separate word and deed as we do, and sometimes the word of God to the prophet was seen rather than heard! (Jer. 1:11, 13).

2 The word is an expression of personality with a power of its own—even a man's word of blessing, once uttered, cannot be recalled, but must have its effect (Gen. 27). God's *dabar* has infinitely greater force: it is His fiat—when God gives the word, things begin to happen (Gen. 1; cf. Ps. 33:6). God's word is dynamic, and can never prove impotent (Ps. 107:20; 147:15ff; Is. 55:10ff).

3 Though God's *dabar* is never personalized, His wisdom (*chokmah*) is, and is represented as a power co-eternal with Him (Job. 28; Prov. 2:3ff; 4:5ff; 7:4; 8:22ff; etc.). This personification becomes even more marked in the Greek Apocrypha, where the creative wisdom tends to be identified with the divine *logos* (Wisd. 9:1; 16:12; Ecclus. 24:3; cf. 2 Esd. 6:38). God's *word* and His *wisdom* are often synonymous, and it is significant that in NT John calls Jesus the Word of God (Jn. 1:1, 14), while Paul calls Him the Wisdom of God (1 Cor. 1:24, 30). The wisdom of God is "an image of His eternal light" (Wisd. 7:26; cf. Jn. 1:4), and, like the Incarnate Word of God, is hated by the world (Prov. 1:28ff; cf. Jn. 1:5, 10, 11).

4 In the Targums (vernacular paraphrases of the OT used in synagogue worship), "word" (Aramaic *memra*) is sometimes used for God Himself—e.g. on Gen. 27:21; "the word of Yahweh should be His God". This is reverential periphrasis rather than a personalization, but it shows that God's word is more than a verbal utterance—it is His creative self-revelation, "the side of God turned towards the world".

THE NEW TESTAMENT

1 As in secular Gk., of statements, declarations, orders (Mt. 19:22; Jn. 2:22; Mt. 8:8), tales or narratives (Mt. 28:15; Acts 1:1; 11:22), questions (Mt. 22:46), reasons, causes (Mt. 5:32), accounts or reckonings (Rom. 14:12; Phil. 4:15; Heb. 4:13), things, affairs (Mt. 21:24; Acts 8:21), etc.

2 Of God's revelation, His commandments, promises, etc. (Mt. 15:6; Jn. 5:38; Rom. 9:6; 13:9; Heb. 2:2).

3 Of the precepts and promises of Jesus (Mt. 7:24; Jn. 14:24), of Christian doctrine generally—i.e. the Gospel (Mk. 4:14–20; Jn. 17:14; Acts 13:46; 2 Cor. 5:19; 2 Tim. 4:2, etc.). As the Divine word comes to men through Christ, "the word", "the word of God", and "the word of Christ" (or "of the Lord") are synonymous.

4 Of Jesus Himself (Jn. 1:1, 14; 1 Jn. 1:1; Rev. 19:13). The word of Jesus which, heard and kept, leads to eternal life, plays a great part in the Fourth Gospel (Jn. 5:24; 8:31, 37, 43, 51f; 12:48; 14:23f; 15:3), and the Prologue explains the power of that word by declaring that Jesus IS what He teaches. Whereas John Baptist, like all the prophets, is but a mouthpiece (Jn. 1:23), Jesus is the very embodiment of the *logos* of God, the expression in a human personality of the Divine light, life, glory and truth (Jn. 1:4, 9, 14). Here John expounds his gospel in current philosophical language. The Greeks explained the universe in terms of *logos*, much as we explain it by "evolution", and John gives the concept a new and higher meaning. As far back as the turn of the sixth century B.C., Heraclitus had used *logos* of the governing principle of Law and Reason in the universe; later the Platonists thought of *logos* as the very basis and essence of reality, while the Stoics spoke of *logos spermatikos*—reason sown like a seed to germinate in the human mind. Already the Jewish philosopher

Philo of Alexandria (b. 20/10 B.C.) had tried to combine these Gk. ideas with the OT doctrine of God's *dabar*, and his teaching had wide currency among educated Jews. St. John goes a stage further: what he is saying in the Prologue is that the *logos* is not a blind, impersonal creative principle or life-force, but the personal expression of the Living God in Jesus Christ—like Paul at Athens, he is revealing to the Greeks their own "unknown God" (Acts 17:23). Here we reach a high-water mark of NT theology: Jesus is not only Messiah, the hope of Israel—He is the very embodiment of God's creative and redemptive purpose, the incarnation of that Word of God[1] which created man and gave him life, now re-creating him for life eternal.

(N. H. Snaith, *The Jews from Cyrus to Herod*; V. Taylor, *The Names of Jesus—Logos*; O. Cullmann, *The Christology of the NT*, 249ff)

---

[1] For the thought of Jn. 1:1-14 in other language, cf. Phil. 2:6ff; Col. 1:15; 2:9; and esp. Heb. 1:1ff.

MATHĒTĒS—DISCIPLE

From the verb *manthanein*, to learn by experience or practice. A related adjective, *mathēmaticos*—fond of learning—gives us the word mathematics. In Gk. literature, *mathētēs* was used of students generally (e.g. of dancing), but especially of the pupils of philosophers and rhetoricians.

THE OLD TESTAMENT
Heb. *talmid*, from *lamad*=to learn.

1 Of scholars in the Temple music school (1 Chr. 25:8). A related word, *limmud* is used in Is. 8:16 of the disciples to whom the prophet entrusted his message, lest it should be lost to posterity.

2 In later Judaism, *talmidim* (disciples) were pupils of the Rabbis, who, like the pupils of the Gk. philosophers, formed schools to perpetuate their masters' teaching. Two of the most famous were the rival rabbinic schools of Hillel and Shammai. Rabbis gathered their pupils around them and taught by question and answer—Lk. 2:46 is typical of the method.

3 This branch of Jewish learning was called *talmud*, a word later used for the great compilations of rabbinic doctrine, *The Talmud*.

THE NEW TESTAMENT
More than 250 times, mostly in the plural, and all in Gospels and Acts.

1 The opposite of *didaskalos* (teacher)—Mt. 10:24; Lk. 6:40.

2 The disciples of the Pharisees (Mt. 22:16; Mk. 2:18; Lk. 5:33), i.e. members of the Pharisaic sect, synonymous with "your sons" (Mt. 12:27).

3 The disciples of Moses (Jn. 9:28), i.e. adherents of the Mosaic Law.

4 The disciples of John Baptist, a group closely attached to their master, even after his imprisonment (Mt. 11:2; Mk. 6:29), and probably continuing long after his death (Acts 19:3ff). Distinguished by observance of special fasts and prayers (Mk. 2:18ff; Lk. 11:1), they had strong views on purification (Jn. 3:25). Two, at least, became disciples of Jesus (Jn. 1:35ff).

5 The disciples of Jesus. The wider circle of His adherents (Lk. 6:13, 17; 19:37; Jn. 4:1; 6; 60f.; 8:31), but especially The Twelve (Mt. 16:13; Mk. 14:32; Lk. 9:14; Jn. 3:22, etc.).

6 In Acts, as the most distinctive term for Christians (6:1, 2, 7; 9:1; 18:23; 19:1; 21:4, 16, etc.): whatever else he is, a Christian is a learner of Christ, one who knows Christ for himself, and can preach, teach (and sometimes heal) in His name. (cf. Mk. 3:14ff).

Every Christian is a disciple (Acts 11:26), bent on the imitation of Christ. Because he knows Him well, he will want to proclaim Him at whatever cost of self-denial and sacrifice (Lk. 14:26, 27, 33), and in this sense, every disciple is also an apostle. *Mathētēs*, then, always retains its original meaning, "learner", but whereas with the disciples of the Gk. sages and the rabbis, it was the master's *teaching* which was all-important, with the Christian, it is the Master's *person*: the disciple is one who lives close to Jesus and who, by his life of love and service, will commend Him to others.

METANOEIN—TO REPENT

Etymologically "to perceive afterwards" or "to think again", "to change one's mind or purpose". Both usages are found, and the orator, Antipho, also frequently uses the verb in the ethico-religious sense, "repent"—its normal meaning in LXX and NT.

THE OLD TESTAMENT

1 The Heb. equivalent, *nacham*, is mostly used of God (i) In morally neutral sense, "change of mind". While God's loving purpose does not change (Num. 23:19; 1 Sam. 15:29; Ps. 110:4), neither is He immutable in the philosophical sense: He varies His action to achieve the ends which human obstinacy and wickedness try to frustrate. Thus He has second thoughts about man (Gen. 6:6) and Saul (1 Sam. 15:35), and takes appropriate action. (ii) Because of His steadfast lovingkindness, God often "repents" (i.e. relents) His threatened punishments (2 Sam. 24:16; Jer. 18:8; Jon. 3:10, etc.). (iii) Once (Jer. 18:10), God is said to "repent" His intended good.

2 While *nacham* is used in Job 42:6 of human repentance, the usual word for this is *shub*—"to turn again", "to turn back". *Shub* is used of men in a bad sense (Jud. 8:33), but commonly denotes true repentance (1 Kgs. 8:35; Neh. 1:9; Is. 31:6; Jer. 25:5; Hos. 12:6): God's good purpose is steady, but man, gone astray in sin, needs to turn back and start again in the path of righteousness. Repentance must be real (Joel 2:13). This is the urgent message of the prophets, but they know that sinful man is powerless to turn and repent. God must turn him and put him in the way; thus even the beginning of salvation is a work of grace (Jer. 31:18; cf. Ps. 51:2, 10; Ezek. 36:26).

THE NEW TESTAMENT

Metanoein occurs some thirty times, and the noun (*metanoia*) is almost as frequent. It is always human repentance, and both verb and noun imply far more than a mere change of mind. (Closely related in meaning is the verb *epistrephein*, "to turn, return or turn towards", corresponding to Heb. *shub*, and used of the turning to God which is repentance (Lk. 1 : 16, 17; Acts 9 : 35; 2 Cor. 3 : 16, etc.).

1 The prophetic exhortation to repentance is taken up with fresh urgency by John Baptist: men must repent because of the imminence of the Kingdom. What is demanded is a complete reorientation of life, therefore even the pious must repent (Mt. 3 : 8ff).

2 Jesus calls for repentance (renunciation of self-confidence) and faith (a fresh start in God-confidence)—Mk. 1 : 15; Lk. 10 : 13; 11 : 32, and these always belong together. So the preaching in Acts (2 : 38; 3 : 19; 17 : 30; 26 : 20) and the Letters to the Churches in Rev. 2 and 3 also enjoin repentance.

3 Because God's requirement of repentance is no legalistic demand (cf. the Pharisees: Mk. 7 : 5ff; Lk. 18 : 9–14), but stems from His redeeming love, the sinner's recovery arouses "joy in heaven" (Lk. 15).

4 Indeed, repentance (like faith) is God's gift (Acts 5 : 31; 11 : 18; Rom. 2 : 4; 2 Tim. 2 : 25)—what theologians call "prevenient grace", the grace which predisposes to conversion.

Salvation begins with repentance: only those who know themselves to be sick have any use for a physician! But it does not end there: repentance leads to faith, and faith to action (Acts 26 : 20; 2 Cor. 7 : 10).

NOMOS—LAW

Usage, custom, law, statute, ordinance, especially of statutes made by authority of the gods or the wisdom of the ancients. In LXX, *nomos* generally translates Heb. *torah* (teaching, law), but sometimes *chuqqah* (decree, statute).

THE OLD TESTAMENT

Heb. *torah*, teaching or guidance which has the authority of a superior—parent (Pro. 1:8), leader (Ex. 18:16), or, especially, God.

1 Of various enactments in legal codes governing ritual and ceremonial matters, as well as public health and private and public morals (Ex. 20:1–17; 20:22–23: 33; 25–31; 34:10–28; 36–40; Lev. 14; 17–26; Num. 1–10; Deut. 5:1–21; 12–26; Ezek. 40–48).

2 In a wider sense, of the Pentateuch (i.e. the whole Mosaic Law and its background), to which all other OT books are secondary (2 Kgs. 14:6; Ps. 119; cf. Acts 13:15).

3 Properly, however, *torah* is wider still; it means the teaching or guidance of God revealed through priest and prophet (Ezek. 7:26)—the whole counsel of God, telling of His nature as well as His requirements, and speaking to the whole life of man, "secular" as well as "religious", as Deut. makes clear.

4 *Torah* is not the means of salvation, but God's word *to those who are already under the grace of the Covenant*: the Covenant is made with Abraham, the Law given to Moses. To suppose, as later Judaism did, that salvation is by keeping the Law, is to put the cart before the horse, and to lapse into the Pharisaic legalism which Jesus condemns.

THE NEW TESTAMENT

1 *Nomos* is used of (i) Law in general (Rom. 3:27; 5:13b)

(ii) Divine laws (Heb. 8:10; 10:16—OT quotations); the law *of Christ* (Gal. 6:2), *of freedom* (Ja. 1:25; 2:12), the *royal law* (Ja. 2:8). (iii) The interior principle of action (Rom. 7:21, 23a, 25). (iv) Mosaic Law (Mt. 5:18; Jn. 1:17; Acts 6:13; Rom. 10:4; 1 Cor. 9:8, etc.). (v) Christian teaching="law of faith" (Rom. 3:27). (vi) The Scriptures, either the Pentateuch (Mt. 12:5; Jn. 1:45), or the OT in general (Jn. 10:34; 1 Cor. 14:21).

2 Jesus regards the Law (summarized in the two commandments of Mk. 12:28-31) as a valid rule of life (Mt. 5:18; Mk. 10:18f; Lk. 10:25ff), but insists that humanitarianism comes before Sabbatarianism (Mt. 12:1-12), and that observance of the commandment must not be substituted for repentance (Lk. 18:9-14).

3 Similarly, Paul approves the Law as good (Rom. 7:7f) and useful as a "tutor unto Christ" (Gal. 3:24) and a curb to the lawless (1 Tim. 1:8).

4 The antithesis between law and spirit (or grace)—Rom. 6:14; Gal. 5:18, is more apparent than real. The Christian must still respect rules of conduct (cf. those in the Epistles: Col. 3; 1 Pet. 2:21ff, etc.): freedom is no excuse for licence (Rom. 6:15ff; 1 Pet. 2:16). The point is that law does not *save*; but as good works, though they do not save, naturally *follow* justification (Col. 3:9ff), so the Christian, saved by grace (not by keeping the law) will thereafter live by law, only now it will be the Law of Love (Jn. 13:34).

(C. H. Dodd, *Moffatt Commentary on Romans*, 34–52, 63–69, 108–114, etc. This vol. is also available in *Fontana Religious Books.*)

ORGĒ—WRATH

Natural impulse, hence temperament, mood, disposition, and so anger, wrath. Common in classical writers, esp. Hesiod, Herodotus.

The chief Heb. words are *aph* (lit. nose, nostril, hence temper, anger—the nostrils quiver in rage!), *chemah* (heat, fury), *charon* (fierceness), *qetseph* (indignation, wrath).

1   OT concerns itself more with the anger of God than of man: Yahweh's anger is kindled against the individual (Ex. 4:14; 2 Chr. 25:15), against idolatrous Israel (Ex. 32:10; Deut. 11:17), against wrong and oppression (Ex. 22:21ff; cf. Amos 2:6ff), and against the nations for their iniquity (Jer. 25:15).

2   Although God's anger is sometimes described anthropomorphically in terms of human sensation (e.g. Ex. 4:14 means lit. "Yahweh's nose burned"—i.e. His nostrils quivered, He snorted), it is essentially different from man's angry outbursts in that it is the steady anger of Him who is "of purer eyes than to behold iniquity", and who can never treat sin lightly.

3   God's anger, terrible as it is, is balanced by His compassion (cf. esp. Ps. 103); even in His wrath, He remembers mercy (Ex. 32:14; Jon. 3:10)—for the penitent, there is always hope.

4   The anger of God can be manifested at any time, but it is especially reserved for the Day of Wrath (Ezek. 7:19; Zeph. 1:15, 18), when the final reckoning with sin will take place.

(HĒMERA—DAY.)

1   *Orgē*[1] and the corresponding verb (*orgizesthai*) are used

[1] (Another Gk. word, *thümos* (passion, hot anger) is used almost synonymously with *orgē* in LXX and NT. Sometimes both occur together (Rom. 2:8; Rev. 16:19; 19:15). As with *orgē*, so with *thümos*, it is God's anger which is chiefly in mind.)

of human anger which, though not necessarily sinful, is not to be nursed (Eph. 4:26), and is deprecated in Christians, especially in bishops (Rom. 12:19; Eph. 4:31; Tit. 1:7).

2   It is attributed to Jesus (Mk. 3:5), but reflects God's righteous indignation, not mere human rage.

3   The noun (but not the verb) is used of God's wrath, rooted in His righteousness, and directed against sin—Rom. 1:18. (It is disputed whether God's *orgē* is an impersonal moral principle, an inevitable process of cause and effect in a moral universe—cf. the verses which follow, or His personal judgment upon evil.)

4   As in OT, God's wrath against sin is matched by His mercy to the sinner: it is not His will that any should perish (Mt. 18:14; Lk. 1:50; 1 Pet. 1:3).

5   Nevertheless, there is a day of reckoning: the NT concept of God's *orgē* is chiefly *eschatological*, looking to the final judgment, the Day of Wrath (Rom. 2:5; Rev. 6:17; cf. Mt. 3:7; Lk. 21:23; 1 Thess. 1:10, etc.), when the repentant will be saved by His mercy (Rom. 5:9), but only the repentant!

OURANOS—HEAVEN

The vault of the heavens, the sky (Hesiod al.); the abode of the gods above the sky (Aeschylus, Plato al.).

THE OLD TESTAMENT
Heb. *Shamayim.*

1   The Hebrews thought of a three-tier universe—a flat earth with *Sheol* beneath and the firmament or sky-vault (possibly supported on pillars at the distant horizon (2 Sam. 22:8; Job 26:11)) arching above (Gen. 1:7ff). In the firmament were suspended the heavenly bodies, sun, moon and stars (Gen. 1:16f; Ps. 19:6; Dan. 12:3): above it dew, rain and snow were stored, to be showered on the earth through the windows of heaven (Gen. 7:11; 27:28; Mal. 3:10; cf. Job 38:22). The heavens are likened to a curtain or tent spread out by God (Is. 40:22).

2   God has His dwelling and throne in Heaven, above the firmament (2 Chr. 30:27; Ps. 11:4; Is. 66:1), and here the angels form a celestial court around Him (1 Kgs. 22:19).

3   Judaism evidently recognized a plurality of heavens (Deut. 10:14; 1 Kgs. 8:27; Ps. 148:4; Neh. 9:6), in the highest of which, "the heaven of heavens", God had His throne. In later Jewish thought, the second heaven was the abode of evil spirits and angels awaiting punishment (cf. Jude 6), and the third heaven was Paradise (cf. 2 Cor. 12:2). The apocryphal books of Enoch detail seven heavens, but the canonical books are more reticent about the celestial sphere.

4   Though Heaven is the fitting home of the high and lofty One, this does not make Him remote. If Heaven is His proper dwelling place, it does not confine His omnipresence, and He dwells also "with him that is of a humble and contrite spirit" (Is. 57:15), but it is not until the Incarnation that the Eternal actually pitches His tent alongside ours (Jn. 1:14).

1 Like Earth, part of God's and Christ's domain (Lk. 10:21; Acts 7:49; 17:24), so that "the heaven and the earth" (Mt. 5:18; Acts 4:24; Rev. 10:6, etc.)=the whole universe. Sometimes, as in later Judaism, *ouranos* is used as a reverential substitute for "God" (Mt. 21:25; Mk. 11:30; Lk. 15:18; Jn. 3:27, etc.)—so in the Gospels, where "Kingdom of God" and "Kingdom of Heaven" are synonymous.

2 Properly, of the realm, high above the Earth, in which God (Mt. 5:16; Rom. 1:18; Rev. 3:12) and the angels (Lk. 2:15; 22:43; Gal. 1:8; Rev. 20:1) dwell. It was from Heaven that Jesus Christ descended at the Incarnation (Jn. 3:13; 6:38; 1 Cor. 15:47), and from there He will come again at the Parousia (Mt. 24:30; 1 Thess. 1:10; 4:16).

3 Though Heaven is distinct from Earth, there is communication between them when God speaks from Heaven (Mk. 1:11; Jn. 12:28), when the Spirit descends (Jn. 1:32; Acts 2:2), or angels appear to men (Mt. 1:20; Lk. 1:26; 24:4 cf. v. 23).

4 Jesus was in the beginning "with God"—i.e. in Heaven (Jn. 1:2; cf. Phil. 2:6), and returned to the celestial region at the Ascension (Lk. 24:51; Acts 1:9f) to sit at God's right hand (Mk. 14:62; 16:19; Rom. 8:34; Heb. 1:3; 8:1). From Heaven He can still speak to men (Acts 9:4ff).

5 Heaven is also the abode of angels, principalities and powers, of "spiritual hosts of wickedness" (Mk. 13:25; Eph. 6:12; Col. 2:10, 15; 1 Pet. 3:22; cf. Rev. 12:7ff) finally to be made subject to Christ.

6 Entered by gates of which Peter is given the keys (Mt. 16:19), Heaven is to be the place of final judgment (Lk. 22:30; Rom. 14:10; 2 Cor. 5:10—though Mt. 25:31f suggests that this is to take place on Earth), and the eternal abode of the righteous who have a truly child-like trust in Christ (Mt. 18:3f; Lk. 6:23; Col. 1:5; 1 Pet. 1:4).

7 Except in Rev., Heaven is not described in detail, but the use of the synonyms *"Abraham's bosom"* (Lk. 16:22ff) and *Paradise* (from a Persian word for a nobleman's park or garden) —Lk. 23:43; 2 Cor. 12:2–4; Rev. 2:7, suggests eternal bliss. In Luke and the Apocalypse, *Paradise* may be either man's final blessed home (Heaven=a return to the Garden of God from which Adam was banished), or the resting place of the righteous

dead prior to the last judgment. In the Pauline text, *Paradise* is clearly the "third heaven". What Heaven will be like, we are not told—only that it will contain the good things which God has prepared for them that love Him (1 Cor. 2 : 9), and that it will be life with God and His Christ (Jn. 14 : 3).

PISTIS—FAITH

Originally active in meaning—trust in others, confidence, assurance, etc., it soon took on also the passive sense—faithfulness, honesty, reliability, means of persuasion, proof, and, in the business world, was used of credit and legal trusts. Sophocles uses the word of religious faith.

THE OLD TESTAMENT

Neither of the two occurrences of "faith" in AV means subjective belief; Deut. 32:20 (Heb. *emun*) is properly translated by RSV "children in whom is no faithfulness", while Hab. 2:4 (Heb. *emunah*) means "the just shall live by his integrity". Here we have the clue: faith is not mere credence, but active trust in the utter dependability of God, and it is this which gives man his only true stability. Three Heb. words express this relationship.

1 *Emunah*—generally "faithfulness" in EVV (the root is *aman*, from which we get "amen"="it is sure"), where the basic idea is the firmness, constancy of God on which men may rely (Ps. 36:5; 89:1; 119:90; Lam. 3:23).

2 *Betach*—confidence, trust, safety (Deut. 33:12; Ps. 4:8; Pro. 1:33; Jer. 23:6).

3 *Chasah*—take refuge, trust (Ps. 7:1; 34:22; 118:8; Is. 57:13). Always peace and security depend upon confidence in God, who is merciful and righteous (Ps. 36:5f; 89:2; Jer. 23:6), and able to fulfil His covenant promises. Trust in men and false gods is of no avail (Is. 30:1–5; 42:17; Jer. 9:4ff).

THE NEW TESTAMENT

By contrast, "faith" is common in all the writings, except the Fourth Gospel, where the verb (*pisteuein*="to believe") is preferred. Faith is the hall-mark of Christians, and the first mem-

97

bers of the Church are called *hoi pisteuontes*—"the believers".
But again, faith is not intellectual assent, but active trust in God
and His Christ.

1 *The Gospels.* The faith that Jesus demands is confident
trust that God is able, through His Messiah, to do what He
promised by the prophets (Mt. 9:4–6; 12:28; Mk. 10:27). This
is the faith (trust in Him, which is accepted as faith in God—Mk.
11:22ff) which enables the lame to walk, etc., and which Jesus
contrasts with fear (Mk. 4:40; 5:36). It is faith in God's mercy
which justifies, not confidence in one's own merit (Lk. 18:9–14).

2 *Paul.* Here faith, which may be "towards God" or "towards
Christ", is contrasted with "works" (Rom. 3:27; Gal. 3:2, 5, etc.).
Christian faith is like that of Abraham—trust in the all-
sufficiency of God, and is unconditional on good works: first the
faith, then the good works which will flow from it.

3 *Hebrews.* Heb. 11:1 gives the only formal definition of
pistis: here the emphasis is on "the unseen reality of God's
present help", and the equally unseen prize for those who endure.
Again, faith is not assent, but trust like that of the Patriarchs.

4 *Peter.* The speech in Acts 2 calls for faith and baptism in
the name of Jesus Christ, the Fulfiller of OT prophecy, who was
crucified and rose again. This is the proclamation (*KERŪGMA*,
q.v.) which is at the heart of all apostolic preaching. Faith in
Christ, crucified and risen, is man's only hope (1 Pet. 1:3).

5 *James.* At first sight this writer contrasts faith unfavourably
with works (2:14, etc.), but closer examination shows that "faith"
here is mere assent to propositions *about* God—a sterile ortho-
doxy to which, of course, good works are clearly superior. On the
other hand, what James calls "works" (2:21, 25) is really the spontaneous expression of true faith in action. His apparent variance
with Paul is one of terminology only, and 5:15 shows that when
thinking of faith in the fuller sense (=trust), his teaching is in
harmony with the rest of NT.

Just as love (*AGAPĒ,* q.v.) is an act of will rather than an
emotion, so *pistis* is no mere effort of intellect, but an act of
self-abnegation, the abandonment of self-reliance (independence
is not a Biblical virtue!). To have faith is to live in unreserved
dependence upon the power and mercy of God.

PNEUMA—SPIRIT

Blast or wind (hence "pneumatic"), breath or breathing, then, metaphorically, the way the wind blows, i.e. prevailing influence. In Plato and Plutarch, sometimes used of divine inspiration.

THE OLD TESTAMENT

Heb. *ruach*, which occurs 378 times in all.

1 Properly, wind or breath—and perhaps, in poetry, the winds were conceived as God's breathing (Ex. 15:8; 2 Sam. 22:16; Ps. 18:15; Is. 59:19). Rarely, God's *ruach* acts on inanimate things—e.g. in creation (Gen. 1:2); more commonly, it is the sustaining power of life (Job. 33:4; Ps. 104:30).

2 The deep breathing of men in anger (Jud. 8:3), grief (Gen. 26:35), zeal (Hag. 1:14).

3 The mysterious power possessing men and producing great feats of strength (Jud. 3:10; 6:34; 13:25; 14:6; 1 Sam. 11:6), qualities of leadership (Num. 11:25; 27:18; Deut. 34:9), wisdom and insight (Gen. 41:38; Pro. 1:23; Dan. 5:14; Ecclus. 39:6), artistic genius (Ex. 31:3), abnormal personality—e.g. insanity (1 Sam. 16:14), and especially the gift of prophecy (Num. 24:2; 1 Sam. 10:5ff; Ezek. 2:2), though the great prophets deprecated the extremer forms of ecstasy.

4 Later, the *ruach* of God is said to be the source of revelation in general (Neh. 9:30; Zech. 7:12), and prophecy looks forward to the coming day when God will pour out His spirit on all men—when all the Lord's people will be prophets (Num. 11:29; Joel 2:28f).

5 A general influence on the whole of man's character (Ps. 51:11).

6 God's living energy in history (Zech. 4:6; 6:8).

7 Of the Lord God, not part of His Being, but the manifestation of His presence among His people (Is. 48:16; Hag. 2:5; cf. Ps. 139:7). This is a high-water mark in OT thought: the spirit of God is not just Divine energy, but God Himself, the Being from whom all power in men and things derives.

1 Though *pneuma* can mean wind (Jn. 3:8a; Heb. 1:7) or breath (2 Thess. 2:8), hence the soul breathed into man (Lk. 8:55; Ja. 2:26; Rev. 11:11), his very self, his *ego* (Rom. 8:16; 2 Cor. 7:1; Col. 2:5), and though it can even be used of evil spirits or demons (Mt. 12:43; Mk. 9:20, etc.), more importantly it is the manifestation of God among and in men, His *Holy Spirit* (Mt. 1:18; Mk. 3:29; Jn. 7:39; Acts 19:2; Rom. 5:5, etc.), for which "Spirit" is often simply an abbreviation.

2 The Spirit, active in creation, and inspiring the prophets, is even more fully present in the preparation for and the birth of Jesus Christ (Mt. 1; Lk. 1): the Spirit identifies Himself with Jesus at the Baptism (Mt. 3:11; Jn. 1:32f), and is the source of Christ's authority and power (Mt. 12:28; Lk. 4:14f; 10:21). In Jesus, because of His sinlessness, the Spirit had full play.

3 In Acts the promise of the Risen Christ is fulfilled (Acts 2), and the confusion of Babel (Gen. 11) removed. The Spirit (always closely linked with the glorified Christ) judges, inspires and warns the Church (Acts 4:8; 9:31; 11:28; 20:28), and, indeed, Acts IS the record of what *the Spirit* achieved through the Apostles.

4 As in the Church corporately, so in its members individually, the Spirit is the source of new life as children of God (Jn. 3:3–8; Rom. 8:14–17). It is the Spirit which ends the inner conflict between "ought" and "can" (Rom. 7:15ff), endows the members of Christ's body with their various gifts (1 Cor. 12:12ff), and produces a harvest of Christian virtues (Gal. 5:22ff). Just as the Spirit confirms the apostolic testimony (1 Jn. 5:6–12; cf. 1 Cor. 12:2f), so He is the source of man's inner strength (Rom. 8:26ff), and the first instalment and promise of our final redemption (Eph. 1:13f).

5 The gift of the Spirit, then, is the consummation of the Incarnation: at Christmas we have God *with* us; at Pentecost, God *in* us (Jn. 14:17). In the life of the Spirit is man's most intimate experience of God in Christ.

(On SOUL and SPIRIT, see H. Wheeler Robinson, *The Christ. Doctrine of Man* (1947), Ch. 1, 2)

PRAOTĒS—MEEKNESS

The adjective *praos* is used of things which are mild—a soft sound, gentle breeze, docile horse, or tame animal. Xenophon uses the neuter of caresses! The noun is used of mildness of disposition, gentleness, the disciplined nature which avoids extremes of passion.

THE OLD TESTAMENT

1 Heb. *anav* describes not so much the self-effacing as the poor and lowly, those in humble circumstances (described in Job 24). These, powerless and despised, can trust only in God, who promises a special blessing upon them (Ps. 22:26; 25:9; 147:6; Is. 11:4; 29:19, etc.).

2 Meekness in this sense became the characteristic of the faithful remnant of Israel, who trusted in God and quietly awaited His consolation (cf. the *Magnificat* (Lk. 1:46–55); Lk. 2:25).

3 Meekness is not, of course, a characteristic of Yahweh, but a great leader like Moses is meek (Num. 12:3), as is the Messiah, even when He comes as King (Zech. 9:9).

THE NEW TESTAMENT

1 Jesus pronounces a blessing on the meek (*hoi praeis*) in Mt. 5:5, and enjoins childlike humility (Mt. 18:2ff). He consistently condemns pride of race (Mt. 8:10–12), sectarian pride and religious ostentation (Mt. 6:5; 23:5; Lk. 18:9ff), and forbids titles of honour to His disciples (Mt. 23:8–10; Mk. 10:35–45). His oral teaching is reinforced by a humble life and by self-effacing actions (Jn. 13:4–17).

2 Paul echoes the condemnation of spiritual pride, personal or racial (Rom. 2:3; 1 Cor. 4:6ff), and repeatedly lists meekness

as a Christian virtue (Eph. 4:2; Col. 3:12; 2 Tim. 2:25, etc.), as do James (1:21; 3:13) and Peter (1 Pet. 3:15).

3 But meekness is not a virtue to be cultivated for its own sake (lest a man pat himself on the back for his humility!)—it is part of the disciple's imitation of Christ, whose meekness is shown not only in His earthly life, but by His condescension in coming to Earth at all (2 Cor. 8:9; Phil. 2:5–11). Man does not *achieve* meekness—his humility is but a faint copy of the humility of Christ and is, like all Christian graces, implanted in his heart by the Holy Spirit (Gal. 5:23; 6:1). Christian meekness is neither the spirit of the humble poor described in OT, nor the tempered spirit admired by the Greeks, but a fusion of gentleness and obedience found in those who have something of the mind of Christ.

PRESBÜTEROS—ELDER, PRESBYTER

Strictly an adjective (the comparative degree of *presbüs*=an old man), *presbüteros* means "older", "senior", hence "an elder", "alderman"—i.e. a senior citizen holding public office, e.g. the president of Sparta. *Presbyterian* (a form of church government in which authority resides in a body of elders) is an Anglicized form of the word.

THE OLD TESTAMENT

Heb. equivalents are:

1 *Malak*, "messenger", "ambassador" (Gen. 32:3; Num. 22:5; 2 Chr. 35:21; Is. 33:7, etc.), where again a senior man is generally in mind.

2 *Zaqen*, "old", "bearded", hence "an elder". Throughout the period elders exercised judicial and administrative functions in Israel (Gen. 50:7; Num. 16:25; Deut. 25:8; 1 Kgs. 8:1; Ezr. 10:8; Ps. 107:32, etc.). In the time of Jesus, members of the Sanhedrin and leaders of local synagogues were "elders" (Mt. 16:21; Lk. 22:52; Acts 4:5, etc.).

THE NEW TESTAMENT

1 Always in Gospels, and sometimes in Acts, of Jewish religious leaders. In Mt. 15:2; Mk. 7:3, 5 (cf. Heb. 11:2), the great religious leaders of the past are meant.

2 In Revelation (4:4; 7:11, 13; 19:4, etc.), *presbüteroi* are those who surround the heavenly throne.

3 Most importantly, in Acts and the Pastoral and General Epistles (though never in the Pauline Epistles proper), *presbüteroi* (pl.) are officials of the Christian Church: (i) Elders were associated with the apostles in the organization of the Jerusalem church (Acts 15:4, 6, 22; 21:18) and elders were also

appointed in the churches founded by Paul and Barnabas (Acts 14:23; 20:17). (ii) According to 1 Tim. 5:17; Ja. 5:14f, their duties are ruling, teaching and pastoral care—e.g. of the sick. Apparently (1 Tim. 4:14; cf. 2 Tim. 1:6; Acts 16:1–4), the *presbüterion* (body of elders) was associated with Paul in the commissioning or ordination of Timothy. (iii) In 1 Cor. 12:28 and Eph. 4:11, Paul lists various functions in the Church, but says nothing of specific offices—e.g. bishop, elder, deacon, and it is likely that these functions were not differentiated in the earliest period. Acts Ch. 6–8 indicate that "the seven" did not confine themselves to table service! (iv) The relation of elder and bishop (*episkopos*, from a verb meaning "to oversee") in apostolic times is disputed. Probably the titles were at first interchangeable (cf. Act. 20:17, 28; 1 Pet. 5:1, 2; Tit. 1:5–7): certainly the monarchical episcopate (i.e. territorial bishops with supreme authority in their respective dioceses) is unknown in NT. (v) Whatever the precise function and status of these officers (and there were others—prophets, evangelists, teachers, etc.), their authority was always *derived*. The apostles derived it by grace and the Spirit from Christ, and others, in turn, derived it by grace and Spirit from them. In the NT, there is but one Head of the Church, Christ, and Church officers exist solely to serve Him and the fellowship.

(J. B. Lightfoot, *Dissertation on the Christian Ministry* (Commentary on Philippians); K. E. Kirk (ed.), *The Apostolic Ministry*; T. W. Manson, *The Church's Ministry*)

PROSEUCHOMAI—TO PRAY[1]

Used only in the religious sense of petition to gods—so
Aeschylus, Herodotus, Xenophon.

THE OLD TESTAMENT

Several Heb. words are used, but without clear distinction. The
most important verb is *palal* which, in the reflexive, means "to
make supplication". The chief noun is *tephillah*="prayer",
"song of praise".

1 Starting from anthropomorphic ideas, e.g. "to smooth God's
face" (Heb. *chalah*—in EVV "beseech": Ex. 32:11; 2 Chr. 33:12,
etc.), and semi-magical notions—"calling upon His name", i.e.
appropriating His power (Heb. *qara*: Gen. 4:26; 2 Kgs 5:11, etc.),
prayer gradually becomes more spiritualized.

2 Private petitionary prayer is offered (1 Sam. 1:10; 1 Kgs.
3:5ff; Dan. 9:20ff, and freq. in Ps.), as are adoration, thanksgiving, confession. In later times, at least, there were set hours of
prayer (Dan. 6:10; cf. Acts 10:9).

3 Great leaders intercede for others—Abraham for Sodom;
Moses, Samuel and the Prophets for Israel (Ex. 32:11; 1 Sam.
12:23; 1 Kgs. 8:23ff; Jer. 14:7ff; Amos 7:5; cf. Job 42:8; Jer. 15:1.)

4 In the early period, prayer was offered, especially at great
festivals, at such local shrines as Shiloh, Mizpah, Gibeon (1 Sam.
1:9ff; 7:5; 1 Kgs. 3:4ff); after Josiah's reforms (2 Kgs. 22–23), *the*
place of prayer was the Temple (Is. 37:14ff., etc.). Exiles prayed
towards Jerusalem (Dan. 6:10). After the destruction of the
Temple (586 BC), prayer was offered in local synagogues.

5 Set forms of prayer are mentioned (Deut. 21:7ff), and many
of the Psalms were used in corporate worship. Believers prayed
standing, kneeling, prostrate, hands uplifted (to receive a blessing), or extended (in entreaty): Gen. 18:22; Neh. 8:6; Ps. 95:6;
Is. 1:15; 45:23; Lam. 2:19.

[1] Other NT verbs, e.g. *deomai* (beseech), *erōtēsai* ("ask for") are included
under this head.

6 Prayer was often accompanied by sacrifice, wearing of sack-cloth, etc., but the important thing in communion with a personal God was seen to be the right disposition of the heart (Ezr. 9:3ff; cf. Pro. 15:8, 29; Joel 2:13).

THE NEW TESTAMENT

1 Jesus habitually communed with God in solitude (Mt. 14:13; Mk. 6:32), and faced all the great crises of life in prayer —Baptism, the calling of the Twelve, the Transfiguration, the Agony, etc. (Lk. 3:21; 6:12f; 9:29; 22:39–46). Prayer often accompanied His miracles (Mk. 7:34; 9:29; Jn. 6:23). He interceded for the disciples (Lk. 22:32; Jn. 17:9ff) and for His executioners (Lk. 23:34).

2 In His teaching on prayer, Jesus stresses the need for privacy (Mt. 6:6), earnestness (Lk. 11:5–13), humility (Lk. 18:9ff), persistence (Lk. 18:1ff), the forgiving spirit (Mt. 6:15), fellowship (Mt. 18:19), faith (Mk. 11:23). Ostentation and verbosity are condemned (Mt. 6:5, 7). Prayer should be in His name (i.e. in conformity with the spirit of Christ)—Jn. 14:13; 16:23. The Lord's Prayer sets the Christian pattern, which is conformity with the Father's will and the promotion of His Kingdom (Mt. 6:9ff; Lk. 11:2–4).

3 In the early church, prayer accompanies baptism (Acts 8:14ff; 19:6), appointment to office (Acts 1:24, 26), healing (Acts 28:8; Ja. 5:13ff), and is part of public worship. (1 Tim. 2). Apostles and converts pray for each other (Rom. 10:1; Phil. 1:4, etc.; Acts 12:5; 2 Cor. 1:11; 2 Thess. 3:1, etc.). Intercession is a general duty (Jas. 5:16), as are confession and thanksgiving (Eph. 5:19f; 1 Jn. 1:9). Christians pray for the return of their Lord (1 Cor. 16:22; cf. Rev. 22:20).

4 Prayer is no mere human activity: often we do not know for what or how to pray, but human deficiency is supplemented by Divine power, for both the Holy Spirit and the Glorified Christ intercede for us (Rom. 8:26, 34; Eph. 6:18; Heb. 7:25).

5 Through Christ we have direct access to God; prayer is now immediate communication needing no human intermediary (Gal. 4:4–7; Eph. 2:18; Heb. 4:15)—God is a Father, freely available to His children.

PROSKÜNEIN—TO WORSHIP

From *künein* to kiss. Frequent in tragedians, Herodotus al. of prostrating oneself before a deity or superior, it describes the attitude of prostration to kiss his feet. In LXX, chiefly for *shachah*.

THE OLD TESTAMENT

The chief Heb. words are *abad*—"to labour, serve" (EVV "worship" in 2 Kgs. 10, elsewhere "serve"), and *hishtahawah* (the reflexive of *shachah*, "to bow down"): for the Hebrew, to worship was to serve. That was why such a grave view was taken of syncretism: to worship idols meant to serve them (cf. Deut. 8:19; 2 Chr. 7:19; Jer. 22:8f, etc.), whereas Yahweh lays exclusive claim to both worship and service (Ex. 20:3ff; Deut. 6:13).

1 In early times, God was worshipped at many local shrines, especially at places like Bethel and Mamre where He was known to have appeared (cf. Ex. 20:24), but later, worship was concentrated at the Jerusalem Temple.

2 Musical instruments (2 Chr. 7:6; Ps. 150:3ff) and levitical choirs (e.g. Asaph and Korah) had their place in the worship, processional psalms were used (the "songs of ascent"), and it is likely that much of the Psalter was chanted antiphonally. Daily sacrifice (see THÜSIA), the celebration of Sabbath and Feasts (Ex. 23:14ff) were liturgically important, as were occasional rites of purification, circumcision, etc.

3 In the course of time, the ritual of worship became more elaborate (cf. the Levitical Code), but there was also a growing awareness, due to prophetic influence, of the importance of inward, spiritual worship (Deut. 11:13; Ps. 40:6; 50:12ff; 96:9; Mic. 6:6ff), and often the spiritual and ritualistic attitudes were in conflict, as they have been in Christianity, especially since the Reformation.

Again, worship is linked with service (Jn. 9:31), and in addition to *proskünein*, we have the verb *latreuein* (from *latris*=a hireling): Lk. 2:37; Rom. 1:9; Rev. 7:15, and its noun *latreia* (Rom. 12:1; Heb. 9:1, 6) as technical terms for the service of God.

1 Jesus observes Jewish feasts (Lk. 22:11; Jn. 7:10), and regularly attends the synagogue (Lk. 4:16), but is not bound by petty Sabbath restriction (Mk. 2:27f), and constantly stresses that the inward disposition is more important than the place or outward form (Mt. 5:23f; Jn. 4:21, 23). Service of one's neighbour is the hall-mark of piety, and as worship is service, practical love of one's fellows is true worship of God (Mt. 25:34–40; Lk. 10:25ff; cf. Ja. 1:27).

2 So also for the apostolic writers, ceremonial and ritual are unimportant, and the observance of holy days, dietary laws, etc., matters of indifference so long as the Christian follows his own conscience and does no violence to the scruples of others (Rom. 14).

3 Of the earliest Christian worship we know little, save that it included prayers, the breaking of bread (Eucharist), psalm singing (Acts 2:42; Col. 3:16), prophetic discourses and ecstatic utterance, and that the first day of the week quickly replaced the Sabbath. Formal liturgies are not prescribed, though orderliness in worship is enjoined (1 Cor. 14:40). Most likely synagogue worship set the pattern for the first Christian services, but specially Christian hymns soon appeared; probably the *Magnificat*, *Benedictus* and *Gloria in Excelsis* were widely used, and some scholars detect other Christian hymns in Eph. 5:14; Phil. 2:6–11; Col. 1:15–20, etc. Extensive use may also have been made of the hand-clasp, the kiss of peace (Rom. 16:16; 1 Pet. 5:14) and of primitive liturgical formulae—e.g. "Our Lord, Come!" and "Jesus is Lord" (1 Cor. 12:3; 16:22; Rev. 20:20). These were the key-notes of worship, which always looked forward to the *Parousia* (1 Cor. 11:26) and final consummation of Christ's Kingdom. It was for this that the early Church prayed (Mt. 6:10) and worked, and both the prayers and the service were part of its ministry.

4 This is reflected in our word "liturgy", which comes from the Gk. *leitourgia*=public service, "ministry" (2 Cor. 9:12; Phil.

2:17, 30), a word in turn derived from *leitourgein*, which means "to discharge a public office at one's own expense". This should provide the clue: the Christian liturgy is no mere ceremonial exercise, but an offering to God involving *service* and *personal sacrifice*. This is the true worship which has *worth* (the Anglo-Saxon was *weorthschipe*) in God's eyes.

PSÜCHĒ—SOUL

(Eng. Psychology)

The life of men (and of animals), especially the conscious self or personality which is the centre of emotions, desires, affections, of thought and moral action. Homer uses *psüche* of ghosts, while Pindar is the first to use it of the immortal soul. Psyche was also the name of a goddess, rival of Aphrodite and lover of Cupid.

THE OLD TESTAMENT
Heb. *nephesh*

1   The principle of life (Gen. 2:7; 35:18) apart from which the body is dead. Thus man *is* a soul (Gen. 46:22), and to seek one's soul (1 Kgs. 19:10; Ps. 35:4) implies murderous intent.

2   The organ of psychical functions: thought (Pro. 2:10), will (Ps. 27:12; Ezek. 16:27), especially emotions—desire, pleasure (Gen. 42:21; Num. 21:5; Deut. 21:14; 23:24; Ps. 78:18).

3   The whole inner life, sustained by the Law (Ps. 19:7).

4   As a personal pronoun=I, me, etc. (Lev. 11:43; Ps. 23:3; 139:14; Ezek. 4:14). *Nephesh* is man's *ego*, his very self, and he is that because of God's breath (i.e. life) within him.

THE NEW TESTAMENT

1   The principle of life (Mt. 6:25; Mk. 3:4; 8:35; Lk. 12:20; Acts 20:10, 24; Phil. 2:30).

2   The inner life, which men cannot destroy (Mt. 10:28).

3   The centre of volitional and emotional life (Mt. 26:38; Lk. 1:46; 12:19; Acts 14:2; Phil. 1:27; 2 Pet. 2:14; cf. Eph. 6:6; Col. 3:23).

4   In one sense the soul, subject to temptation (1 Pet. 2:11) and needing to be kept pure (1 Pet. 1:22), watched over by Apostles and bishops (2 Cor. 12:15; Heb. 13:7) is the most

precious part of man (Mt. 16:26). In another sense, since even unbelieving men have souls, there is a contrast between the purely psychical and the higher, pneumatic (=spiritual) life peculiar to Christians (1 Cor. 2:14, 15; 15:44-46). The point is that men are souls *to be saved* (Ja. 1:21; 5:20): the soul is the object of Divine grace. As it was God's breath which made him a living soul, so it is God's power again which gives him life eternal. (See *Pneuma*—Spirit)

SARX—FLESH

Properly the soft tissues; sometimes=the whole body. Epicurus spoke of it as the seat of the affections and passions, and in Hellenistic thought of NT times *sarx* was often little more than man's base animal nature.

THE OLD TESTAMENT
Heb. *basar*

1 Animal food (=meat)—Lev. 7:15; Dan. 10:3. Man's soft tissues (Gen. 17:23; Ezek. 37:8).

2 Physical nature (men or other animals), the seat of pain and pleasure (Job. 4:15; Ps. 16:9; 119:120; Eccles. 2:3; 12:12), as contrasted with God's spiritual being (Gen. 6:3; 2 Chr. 32:8; Job 10:4; Is. 31:3).

3 Kinship—man and wife, family, tribe, etc. (Gen. 2:23ff; 37:27). "All flesh"=humanity (Ps. 65:2; Is. 58:7; Joel 2:28).

4 Flesh is mortal, weak and erring and requires God's forbearance (Job 4:17–19; Ps. 78:39f; cf. Ps. 103:14).

5 Man as created is essentially flesh, therefore flesh cannot be essentially sinful; indeed, it is capable of spiritual longing (Ps. 63:2; 84:2).

6 But, in fact, man early became corrupt (Gen. 6:13; cf. Gen. 3). His fall was due, however, to his spiritual pride, not his material origin.

THE NEW TESTAMENT

1 Of animal tissue (1 Cor. 15:39, 50; 2 Cor. 12:7).

2 Human nature, humanity (Mk. 13:20; 1 Cor. 1:29; cf. 2 Cor. 5:16, RSV); kinship (Rom. 9:3).

3 Christ's sacrifice (Jn. 6:52–6).

4 Man's physical as opposed to spiritual nature (1 Cor. 5:5;

1 Pet. 3:18)—thus *works* (Gal. 5:19ff), *mind* (Rom. 8:7) of the flesh, i.e. the sinfulness rooted in human self-centredness.

5 Though man is torn by warring flesh and spirit, his flesh is not itself evil, and through His Incarnation (L. in+caro, carnis=flesh) and Passion, Christ conquered sin in the flesh (Rom. 8:3).

6 Through Christ's victory, believers have crucified the flesh (rebellious human nature), and live by and for the Spirit (Gal. 5:24).

(C. A. Anderson Scott, *Christianity According to S. Paul*, 34ff. H. Wheeler Robinson, *The Christian Doctrine of Man*, 24f; 113ff)

SOPHIA—WISDOM

Properly of skill in handicrafts, arts and science (from carpentry to music and surgery), hence skill in human affairs, shrewdness, sagacity (cf. "sophistication")—even craft, cunning. Aristotle lists *sophia* (speculative wisdom) as one of the three intellectual virtues.

THE OLD TESTAMENT

1   Heb. *chokmah* is practical and theological rather than theoretical and philosophic: it can be used of technical proficiency (Ex. 35:30ff; Is. 10:13; cf. Ezek. 27:8), and as it is the opposite of folly (which is *culpable* stupidity—1 Sam. 26:21; cf. Ps. 14:1), it is a branch of piety.

2   So, in the days of the kingdom, "the wise" are a professional guild (from whom the later "scribes" may have been descended) parallel with the priests and prophets (Is. 19:12; Jer. 8:8; 18:18). Solomon was the wise man *par excellence.*

3   "The wise" produced an extensive wisdom literature—Job, Prov., Eccles., Dan. and some Psalms, and in Apocrypha, Wisd., Ecclus.

4   God's wisdom is demonstrated especially in the creation of the universe and man (Ps. 104:24; Pro. 17:15f; Is. 40:13f) and all human wisdom is His gift to the obedient (Deut. 4:6; Job 28:28).

5   The personification of wisdom as a pre-existent divine agent (Pro. 8; cf. Wisd. 7:22–27; Ecclus. 24:3–22) bore fruit in NT Christological teaching—Jn. 1:1–14; Col. 1.

THE NEW TESTAMENT

1   Jesus commends human sagacity and foresight (Mt. 10:16; 24:45; Lk. 16:8), within its limitations.

2   Some things are hid from self-centred human wisdom (Lk.

10:21; Ja. 3:13–15), and for true enlightenment a spiritual wisdom (Lk. 21:15; Acts 6:3, 10; Col. 1:28; Ja. 3:17; 2 Pet. 3:15) is needful.

3 This higher knowledge stems from God's unsearchable wisdom (Rom. 11:33; 1 Cor. 2:7), often contradictory to commonsense judgments (1 Cor. 1:21–24), and is given through the indwelling of the Spirit or of Christ (Eph. 1:17; Col. 3:16).

4 In short, the love of Christ is the beginning of Christian wisdom.

(E. Jacob, R. Mehl, *Vocab. of the Bible*, 451ff)

SŌTĒRIA—SALVATION

Classical usage: Quite generally of deliverance, preservation, means or guarantee of safety, also medically of bodily health.

THE OLD TESTAMENT

The root meaning of Heb. words *yeshuah, yesha, teshuah* is "to be broad, spacious: to be unconfined and at ease". Salvation may be from a perilous situation (Ex. 14:13; Deut. 20:4; 1 Sam. 14:45) or from sickness or moral anguish etc. (Ps. 6:4; 69:1). Personal salvation from sin and guilt is rare (Ps. 51:14).

1 Salvation is accomplished by human saviours (Jud. 3:9-15), but as Divine agents. Only Yahweh is an absolute saviour (Ps. 3:8; 33:16ff; Is. 45:21; Jer. 3:23; Hos. 5:13).

2 Though salvation is social (even nationalistic) and concrete, there are requirements of penitence and righteousness (Ps. 119:115; Is. 45:8).

3 In Messianic teaching, salvation becomes more spiritual (Jer. 31:31ff; Ezek. 36:26ff; Hos. 14), and more universal (Is. 52:10): it is from sin and guilt that all men need to be saved. Apocalyptic writings look for final salvation in a new Messianic age through a resurrection of those who have passed through judgment (Is. 65:17; Dan. 7; 12), and these eschatological and apocalyptic ideas are echoed in NT.

THE NEW TESTAMENT

1 The verb (*sōdzein*) is commoner than the noun: salvation is active, what God has done and is doing. It is appropriated through faith (Eph. 2:8).

2 Salvation may be from sickness, peril, death, etc. (Mt. 8:25; 9:21; Acts 27:20), but more especially it is the gospel (Rom. 1:16), including redemption, justification, forgiveness etc.,

whereby man passes from sin and darkness to peace and fellow-ship with God (Lk. 1:77; Jn. 5:24; Gal. 5:1; Eph. 1:7; 2:12f; 1 Pet. 2:10; 1 Jo. 5:12).

3 It is present—believers are already being saved (1 Cor. 15:2; 2 Cor. 6:2; Ja. 1:21), but its consummation is still a hope to be realized after judgment on the last day (Rom. 13:11; 1 Pet. 1:5; Heb. 1:14).

4 All salvation is through Jesus Christ (Acts 4:12; Rom. 5:9f): for this He was born (Mt. 1:21), and for this He died (Heb. 5:8f).

THEOS—GOD

God, the Deity—of pagan gods and goddesses, and of Roman Emperors accorded divine status after death. In LXX, chiefly for *el, elohim*.

THE OLD TESTAMENT

1 Several names for God are used: (i) *El* ("power" or "strong one"). Used of the God of Israel, sometimes (e.g. Is. 44:17) of other gods. Often compounded with other names or titles—*El Shaddai* (RSV "God Almighty": Gen. 17:1); *El Roi* ("a God of seeing": Gen. 16:13), and found in proper names—e.g. *El*iakim ("May El raise up"), Ezeki*el* ("May El strengthen"). (ii) *Elohim*, the ordinary Heb. word for God (Gen. 1:1; Ex. 2:23; Deut. 4:3; Jud. 6:39; Ps. 14:2; Is. 40:3; Jer. 7:23, etc.). (iii) *Yahweh* (EVV, THE LORD; LXX gen. *kürios*), means probably "I am who I am" (RSV). (The Eng. form Jehovah is a barbarism compounded of the consonants of *Yahweh* and the vowels of *adonai* ("my Lord"), and dates only from medieval times.) (iv) The shortened form, *Yah* occurs alone (Ex. 15:2; Ps. 77:11 and freq.; Is. 12:2, etc.), in names such as Jehoiakim ("May Yah raise up"), Azariah (Yah has helped), and in the ejaculation *Hallelujah* ("praise ye Yah"). (v) *Yahweh Sabaoth* (common esp. in the prophets)— "The Lord of Hosts"—i.e. of the armies of Israel (Yahweh a war God: 1 Sam. 17:45) or of the host of stars or legions of spirits and angels. This title emphasizes God's active rôle in history.

2 Strange (pagan) gods, the *baalim* (pl. of *baal*, "lord", "master"), and the goddess, *Ashtoreth* (Jud. 10:6; 1 Sam. 7:4) are mentioned. These are no gods and cannot save (1 Kgs. 17–18; Is. 40:19; 45:20; Jer. 16:20).

3 Before Josiah's reforms, syncretism was common (1 Kgs. 11:7–23; cf. 2 Kgs. 23:13), and the complaints of later prophets prove that idolatry persisted long after. In popular religion,

Baal's qualities, and sometimes his name, were attached to Yahweh, as such Heb. personal names as Yerubbaal, Eshbaal, Baalyada, etc. indicate.

4 Official Hebrew teaching, however, is uncompromisingly monotheist: Yahweh is sole Creator of the universe, and His existence, recognized by all right-thinking men, needs no proof. Because He is the only God, He scarcely needs a personal name, and in later usage, "The Name" is not spoken—He is simply *Adonai*—Lord.

If we owe philosophy and art to the Greeks, commerce to the Phoenicians, law to the Romans, we certainly owe religion to the Hebrews, for they alone of ancient peoples knew God.

THE NEW TESTAMENT

1 No new doctrine of God appears: *Ho Theos* is Yahweh, the God of the Law and the Covenants, who spoke by the prophets (Mt. 22:32; Mk. 12:29–32; Acts 17:24ff; 1 Cor. 8:4; 10:20; Heb. 11:6)—all that is new is the fuller revelation of Him in the face of Jesus Christ (2 Cor. 4:6).

2 *The relation of God and Jesus.* (i) Jesus habitually speaks of God as other than Himself (Mk. 10:9, 18; 13:19; 15:34); He exercises Divine power (Lk. 11:20) but disclaims Divine omniscience (Mt. 24:36) and refuses to invoke Divine omnipotence (Mt. 4:1-10; 26:53). (ii) On the other hand, Jesus claims a uniquely intimate relationship with God (Mt. 11:25-27; Lk. 10:21f; Jn. 10:30; 14:9) and to be the sole means of access to the Father (Jn. 14:6). (iii) Jesus is "Son of God", "the Son", "His Son", "the Only Begotten Son": He obviously believed Himself to be the Son of God in a pre-eminent sense, and the whole NT indicates that "Son of God" was a title commonly used of Him in the early Church. (iv) Jesus is also called the "image" (2 Cor. 4:4; Heb. 1:1–3), "power" and "wisdom" of God (1 Cor. 1:24), etc. In Jn. 20:28; Tih. 2:13 and perhaps Rom. 9:5 (where punctuation is determinative—see AV, RV against RVm, RSV, NEB), Jesus is called *Theos*—God. In the Johannine Prologue, the creative *Logos* which becomes flesh in Jesus is *Theos* (Jn. 1:1), while Phil. 2:6 says Jesus was originally in the form (*morphē*) of God. Though NT writers do not generally call Jesus God in

so many words, the Divinity of Jesus is clearly basic to their thought.

3 Thus, though the NT contains no new *doctrine* of God, it presents a more complete revelation of Him (Jn. 14:9; Heb. 1:1ff). Jesus is *Emmanuel*, God with us (Mt. 1:23); in Him all our ideas of God are brought to focus, and the remote Deity comes near. Jesus came "to put a face on God".

4 As in OT, God is no mere "Ultimate Reality" or "Ground of Being", but a Personal Saviour-God, whose demands upon men are exclusive (Mt. 5:48; 6:24; Lk. 12:19ff), and therefore His Son, Jesus, will have nothing less than a whole-hearted response of faith and obedience (Mt. 10:37; Lk. 9:62; cf. Lk. 5:28). In Christ the revelation of God is complete and the claims of God are absolute.

THŪSIA—SACRIFICE

From the verb *thuein*, "to offer". Used by Empedocles, Herodotus, Pindarus, Plato al. of sacrifices made to the gods.

THE OLD TESTAMENT
Sacrifice, which was central to Israelite religion from the earliest times, was regarded as a gift to God, a means of fellowship with Him and with men, and a mode of releasing life. It was the *life* of the victim, residing in its blood, which was offered to God—not the animal's dead body (cf. Gen. 9:4). Sacrifices were offered on annual feast days (Lev. 23:37ff; cf. 1 Sam. 20:6), at the time of the various harvests (Lev. 23:10ff), to ratify a treaty (Gen. 31:54), in thanksgiving for deliverance (Gen. 8:20). In addition there were the morning and evening sacrifices made daily for king and people (1 Kgs. 18:29, 36; 2 Kgs. 16:15). Although there were many different types of sacrifice, three are specially important:

1 *Olah* (lit. "that which ascends"), a burnt offering, generally public, offered on certain stated occasions (Ex. 29:38ff; Lev. 1). Private offerings, votive or free-will, might also be made. The victim was to be spotless, but the poor might give small animals (Lev. 1:14).

2 *Shelem* (peace offering—cf. *shalom*=peace)—Ex. 24:5; Lev. 3:1; Deut. 27:7; Ezek. 45:15, 17), intended to promote peaceful relations with God, often a private sacrifice, and often a thanksgiving for benefits received or anticipated. Small animals (even imperfect in the case of a free-will offering) might be used. (Lev. 22:23). Part only of the animal was burnt, part went to the priest, the rest was eaten by the sacrificer and his friends as a communion meal.

3 *Chattath*—sin offering (Lev. 4:1–5:13) and *asham*—guilt offering or trespass offering (AV)—Lev. 5:14–6:7; 1 Sam. 6:3;

Ezek. 40:39; cf. Is. 53:10. Although, at least after the Exile, all sacrifices were thought to have atoning power, *chattath* and *asham* were the expiatory sacrifices proper. Even so, they were a remedy only for unwitting sin (ritual offences and the like): for deliberate sin ("presumptuous sin", "sin with a high hand") they were not effective (Num. 15:29f; Ps. 19:13; cf. Heb. 10:26–31). True, these offerings were sometimes associated with cases of theft or misappropriation, but there the offender had to make full reparation plus 20 per cent, and offer his sacrifice to boot!

The Exile deepened Israel's sense of sin, and the pious, influenced by the prophets, came to see that while sacrifices might be useful enough as an outward sign of righted wrongs, sin's damage to the soul could be repaired only by God. Between a man and his God, the only effective sacrifice is a broken and contrite heart (Ps. 51:17; Pro. 21:3; Is. 55:7; 58:6–9; Mic. 6:6–8; Dan. 4:27). The ritual of sacrifice continued until the destruction of the Temple in A.D. 70, when it ceased altogether. By then, the only true atoning sacrifice was available to men!

THE NEW TESTAMENT

1 *Jesus* does not sweepingly condemn the sacrificial system; indeed (Mt. 8:4 and parallels), He bids the cleansed leper make the offerings required by the Law (Lev. 14:2–32) *for a testimony unto them.* He recognized the value of sacrifices as an outward sign, but Mt. 9:13; 12:7; cf. 23:23 show that He could never allow them as a substitute for a right disposition of the heart towards God. The Scribe in Mk. 12:33 rightly interpreted His mind. In any case, sacrifices belong to the Old Dispensation; as Christ is greater than the Temple, the seat of sacrifice (Mt. 12:6), so the New Covenant which He inaugurates (Mt. 26:26–29; Lk. 22:15–20; Mk. 14:22–25) is superior to the Old, and His sacrifice more efficacious than the sacrifices of Israel.

2 *Paul* says little about the sacrificial system, but uses its terminology when he sees his own death as a libation poured out upon the sacrifice of the Philippians' faith (Phil. 2:17) and exhorts the Romans to "present their bodies (i.e. lives) a living sacrifice" (Rom. 12:1). The language of sacrifice occurs again in Rom. 15:16, where the *offering* he brings (the word is *prosphora*) is that of his Gentile converts. Sacrifice for Paul, as for Peter

(1 Pet. 2:5) is spiritual, not material—the logical development of OT thought (e.g. Ps. 40:6ff; Is. 1:11ff; Amos 5:21ff).

3 *Hebrews.* Although the sacrificial nature of Christ's death appears elsewhere (Jn. 1:29; Rom. 3:24f; Eph. 5:2; Rev. 5:6–9), its full development is here (esp. ch. 9, 10), where the thought background is the Day of Atonement (Lev. 16). What Jewish sacrifice could never do—i.e. atone for sin (Heb. 9:9; 10:1, 4, 11), the Mediator of the "better covenant" (Heb. 8:6) effects. The contrast is pointed. The High Priest entered a Holy of Holies made with hands; Christ entered the heavens to make atonement (9:24). The Priest performed the rite annually; Christ once for all (9:25f; 10:10–12). The Priest, a mortal, sinful man, offered for his own transgression; Christ, the sinless Son of God, makes atonement only for others (7:26). Above all, whereas the High Priest offered the blood of animals, Christ offered Himself (9:14; 10:10). OT sacrifice was offered for the sins of the man who brought it; the sacrifice of Christ, freely offered, avails for the sins of all. This is the only true sacrifice, eternally valid, unlimited in scope, and it is God's gift! Men's sacrifice may signify thanksgiving or betoken penitence, but it cannot *buy* forgiveness. ForGIVEness must always be given! The OT saints, as we have seen, recognized this: they knew that "to obey is better than sacrifice" (1 Sam. 15:22), but it was precisely obedience of which they were incapable! (cf. Rom. 7:22–24). What man could not offer, God *gave* in Christ, in whom obedience and sacrifice were joined.

ZŌĒ—LIFE

Classical Gk. had two words for life, *zōē* and *bios*; the poets used them synonymously, but, strictly speaking, *zōē* was the physical life common to man and animals (hence, *zoo*logy), while *bios* denoted mode of life, manner of living (mostly of men)—hence our *bio*graphy). NT takes the inferior word, *zōē* and fills it with spiritual meaning. *Bios*, too, occurs, but only ten times, and then in the sense, duration or course of life (Lk. 8:14; 1 Tim. 2:2; 1 Jn. 2:16 etc.), or living, livelihood, means (Mk. 12:44; Lk. 8:43 etc.).

THE OLD TESTAMENT

1   The common Heb. equivalent is *chaiyim* (pl.), not mere existence, but fulness of life. True life is possible only to them who obey God's will (Pro. 3:1–10) and His wisdom (Pro. 3:18; 13:14) and follow in the way of righteousness (Pro. 12:28, etc.). Disobedience is the road to death (Deut. 30:15ff). The Living God (Ps. 42:2; Dan. 6:26, etc.), active in His world, creating, guiding, punishing and delivering man (Deut. 32:39; Is. 57:15ff; Neh. 9:6), is the source of all life (Gen. 2:7; Job 10:12) and full life is possible only in relation to Him (Deut. 8:3).

2   Another Heb. word often rendered "life" is *nephesh*, strictly "breath" or "soul"—e.g. Ex. 4:19: "all the men are dead which sought thy *nephesh*". For the Hebrew, the soul is life and flows from God—cf. 1 Sam. 25:29: "the soul (*nephesh*) of my Lord (David) shall be bound in the bundle of life (*chaiyim*) with the Lord thy God". Other metaphors used of life are the tree (Gen. 2:9), path (Ps. 16:11), fountain (Ps. 36:9), book (Ps. 69:28), light (Ps. 56:13; cf. Job 33:30), the land of the living (Ps. 27:13).

THE NEW TESTAMENT

Zōē is used in a double sense:

1   Of this transient, earthly life, given by God (Acts 17:25),

and terminated at death (Mk. 5:23; Phil. 1:20; Ja. 4:14). Man is responsible to God (or Christ) for the use he makes of it (Rom. 14:7, 10; 2 Cor. 5:10; 1 Pet. 4:5), and God who has given it may withdraw or destroy it at will (Lk. 12:20; cf. Mt. 10:28).

2 In the light of the Resurrection and the gift of the Spirit, *zōē* is used of a higher kind of life, *eternal life,* by contrast with which our natural, sin-ridden existence is nothing but death (Col. 2:13; 1 Tim. 5:6). Eternal life is the gift of God through Christ (Jn. 10:28; 1 Jn. 5:11); Christ is the Prince (Acts 3:15), bread (Jn. 6:35) and water of life (Jn. 4:10; Rev. 21:6). Variously described as "life in the Spirit" (Gal. 6:8), "life in Christ Jesus" (Rom. 5:17; 6:23; 2 Cor. 4:11), or simply "newness of life" (Rom. 6:4), it is apprehended by faith (Jn. 20:31): to know Him is to have eternal life as a present possession, not just a future hope (Jn. 17; esp. 5:24), and those who have it are free from sin and death (Rom. 8:2). But, as always, faith involves the works of love (cf. 1 Jn. 3:14)—eternal life is given to those who are worthy (Mt. 25:46; Lk. 10:28; Jn. 5:29; Rom. 2:7; cf. Mt. 7:13f). Though eternal life is a present reality, because it involves growth and development, its full glory is yet to appear (Col. 3:4). It begins here, but the best is yet to come (cf. Mk. 10:29f).

DIATHĒKĒ—COVENANT

Covenant is treated here as representing not one important theological concept among many, but the fundamental relationship of loyal love between God and man upon which the other Biblical doctrines depend and in which they find their coherence.

In the classical period the word meant *compact* or *contract*, but in Hellenistic Greek (the common language of New Testament times), it came to mean exclusively *last will and testament*, and *diathēkē* is so used in Gal. 3:15ff and Heb. 9:16f. Generally, however, *diathēkē* in the NT retains the Septuagint (LXX) meaning *covenant, decree, declaration of purpose.* The Heb. word *berith* (probably derived from a word for 'bond' or 'fetter') is extremely common in the OT, where it is used mostly of Yahweh's covenant with Israel. LXX translated *berith* by *diathēkē* rather than *sünthēkē* because the former does not imply equality between the parties; the Bible always insists that the covenant is not something man negotiates (like an agreement or treaty —that would be *sünthēkē*) but something God commands (Jos. 7:11), establishes (Lev. 26:9), makes (Deut. 5:2) or gives (Acts 7:8). The initiative is always with God: the covenant is a covenant of *grace*, and we are always the recipients.

THE OLD TESTAMENT

1 *Between man and man. Berith* is used of covenants between individuals (Gen. 21:27), tribes (Ex. 23:32; Deut. 7:2), king and people (2 Kgs. 11:4; 2 Chr. 23). Such covenants were sealed by gifts, handshakes, kisses, common meals or sacrifices (Ezek. 17:18; 2 Sam. 3:17-21; Gen. 31:44ff).

2 *Between God and man.* (1) *Berith* is used of Yahweh's covenant with Israel, made on Horeb-Sinai (Ex. 19), though earlier covenants with Abram (Gen. 15:18) and even Noah (Gen. 9:8-17) indicate that, though formally made with Israel at Sinai, the covenant applies to all humanity (cf. Ecclus. 17:12). The Sinai covenant, sealed by sacrifice ("the blood of the covenant"—Ex. 24:8; Zech. 9:11), was the basis of Hebrew religion, and to it the prophets constantly hark back (Jer. 7:23f; Hos. 8:1). (2) The covenant confers privileges on Israel as the chosen people, but also involves obligations: the promises are *to such as keep his covenant and . . . remember his commandments to do them* (Ps. 25:10; 103:18). Here *berith* is almost synonymous with "the Law", and indeed in Ex. 24:7 the commandments of God are called "the Book of the Covenant" (Ex. 20:22-23:33). Because the Book of the Covenant reposed in the Ark of the Covenant (Deut. 10:1-8), the latter was exceedingly precious: to lose it in battle (i.e. to lose God's promises) was a disaster for Israel—see 1 Sam. 4, esp. v. 22. (3) Circumcision was the physical mark of belonging to the covenant people

(Gen. 17:9ff; cf. Acts 7:8), and Paul sometimes refers to the Jews simply as "the circumcision" (Gal. 2:8; Tit. 1:10). Conversely, the heathen are "the uncircumcised" (Jud. 15:18; 2 Sam. 1:20; Jer. 9:25f). (4) The formal, written covenant proved altogether too external and legalistic, and so the prophets look forward to a new, spiritual covenant[1] written in men's hearts (Jer. 31:31ff)—i.e. a covenant men will *want* to obey because their hearts are in it. Like the old covenant, the new one will involve purification (Mal. 3:1ff), for only so will Israel become fit to be in covenant with a God of holiness.

THE NEW TESTAMENT

Redemption is a continuing process brought to its culmination at the Incarnation. The covenant is not set aside, but gloriously fulfilled and expanded: the new, spiritual covenant looked for by the prophets is established in Christ, and the Greek name for the NT is *HĒ KAINĒ DIATHĒKĒ*—"The New Covenant".

1 *The Gospels and Acts.* (i) The Song of Zacharias (Lk. 1:68ff) takes up the OT ideas of covenant—the merciful initiative of God, His loyal care for His people, and His demand for their obedience. Acts 3:25 extends the covenant benefits to all mankind as was originally intended in the promise to Abram. (ii) In the Gospels the Kingdom ("of heaven" or "of God") is the equivalent of the covenant relationship, and demands the same exclusive obedience: at the Last Supper, Jesus speaks both of "appointing a kingdom" (Lk. 22:29) and of instituting a "new covenant" in His own blood (Lk. 22:20; 1 Cor. 11:25; cf. Heb. 12:24). Both covenant and kingdom imply Divine sovereignty and our obligation to God in loyalty and service.

2 *Paul and Hebrews.* The new covenant is a better covenant from God (Heb. 7:22; 8:6) bringing forgiveness to the sons of promise (Rom. 9:8). It is also wider, as embracing Gentiles as well as Jews (Rom. 9:24ff). As *faith* only was the condition upon which God granted His covenant to Abram, so it is the sole requirement of the new covenant. Works and circumcision are quite beside the point (Rom. 2:28f; 11:6; Gal. 2:16; 5:6). The covenant is not of bondage, but of freedom (Gal. 4:24ff)—i.e. not of law but of love. Moreover, it is a covenant that knows no end (Heb. 13:20).

Covenant, then always keeps both its main senses: it is a *disposition* made freely by God, without any thought of our worthiness. It is also a *bond*—God has bound Himself by His word. God's favour to men is not intermittent and chancy but constant, dependable and eternal. But if God is bound, so are we—bound in the service in which we realise our only perfect freedom.

[1] The Dead Sea Scrolls (*Zadokite Documents*; *Habakkuk Commentary*) show that the Qumrân sect was greatly influenced by this idea. The community's *Manual of Discipline* contains solemn covenant ceremonies which stress the inward qualities of loyalty, love, truth. Evidently, like the young Church in Acts, the sect thought of itself as the community of the new covenant.

INDEX